Prison
Letters

First published: March 1981
This edition: 2019
Copyright © John Jenkins & Y Lolfa Cyf., 1981

ISBN: 978-1-912631-13-1

Cover photograph: Robat Gruffudd (taken at the site of
Capel Gwladys, described in the letter to Cyril Hodges,
22 December, 1971)
Back cover photograph: © John Jenkins

Printed and published in Wales
by Y Lolfa Cyf., Talybont, Ceredigion SY24 5HE
e-mail ylolfa@ylolfa.com
website www.ylolfa.com
tel. 01970 832 304

Prison Letters

John Jenkins

Edited by Rhodri Williams

PORTMEIRION SHOPS

WALES MILLENIUM CENTRE,

M***10424   TID*****161
AID : A0000000031010
Visa Debit

VISA DEBIT

**** **** **** 7325
CONTACTLESS   PAN SEQ 0
SALE

CARDHOLDER COPY

AMOUNT   £9.9

No CVM Used
14:04 22/10/19
AUTH CODE: 9144C

Foreword

On the second of November 1969 a hitherto unknown army officer, John Barnard Jenkins, was arrested by police investigating a three-year bombing campaign and charged with a variety of offences involving explosives. Following his trial at the Flintshire Assizes, Mold he was sentenced to ten years imprisonment by Mr Justice Thompson, the greater part of which he served as a category 'A' prisoner in the maximum security prison at Albany, Isle of Wight. Despite the fact that the bombing which had overshadowed Welsh political life since 1967 was over, the name of John Jenkins was soon to become one of the most potent in Welsh politics. Feared by the authorities and the establishment, as was clearly demonstrated by the judge's remarks when passing sentence, and respected by nationalists of all persuasions, including devout pacificts, John Jenkins served almost seven years of his sentence. He was released on the 15th of June, 1976 and despite his subsequent withdrawal from active politics of any kind he remains an enigmatic presence within Welsh politics.

Born of English-speaking parents in Cardiff in 1933, John Jenkins was brought up in the village of Penybryn in the Rhymney Valley. Educated at Bargoed Grammar School, he joined the Army in 1952 and served with the Royal Army Dental Corps in Austria and Germany. Despite his promotion to the rank of sergeant he left the Army at the end of his first term and returned to the Rhymney Valley and worked in a steelworks and a coalmine before being involved in a motor-cycle accident which put him in hospital. On recovery he stayed on to work at the hospital where he met his future wife, but in order to be able to afford to get married he rejoined the Army in 1958 and took up his former position as a Sergeant in the Royal Army Dental Corps. His first tour abroad took him to Cyprus where he witnessed the campaign for independence, the return of Archbishop Makarios from exile and the first years of independence, all of which had a profound influence on his political thinking. Following a second tour of Germany John Jenkins eventually returned to Wales in 1964 and was stationed at Saighton Camp in Chester and lived in married quarters at Wrexham until his arrest in 1969.

The Wales to which John Jenkins returned in 1964 was in many ways different from the country he left in the late fifties. Despite unanimous opposition in Wales Liverpool Corporation's proposals for the drowning of Capel Celyn and Cwm Tryweryn were approved by Parliament. Plaid Cymru, under the leadership of Gwynfor Evans, refused to take up direct action and by April 1963 those who had undertaken such action, Emyr Llewelyn, John Albert Jones and Owain Williams, were all in prison. Plaid Cymru's opposition to the proposals to build another reservoir at Clywedog shortly afterwards achieved nothing. The party was, it is true, on the verge of achieving its best electoral results to date in the by-elections of the late sixties —Gwynfor Evans winning Carmarthen in July 1966, Vic Davies and Phil Williams coming within 2,000 votes of the Labour victors at Rhondda West in March 1967 and Caerffili in July 1968 respectively —but John Jenkins, like many other of the younger generation of nationalists was acutely aware of the political impotence of Plaid Cymru and the Welsh people. (It should be remembered that the bombing campaign which was to continue until 1969 began before Gwynfor Evans' victory at Carmarthen in July when a cable tower at the site of the Clywedog reservoir was destroyed by an explosion on March the 7th 1966. Plaid Cymru's subsequent failure in the General Election of 1970 cannot simply be attributed to the activities of M.A.C.).

Something was needed to raise the political consciousness of the people of Wales: something that would force people to think about the conditions under which they lived. As is made perfectly clear in the letters, it was not M.A.C.'s aim to secure short-term political conscessions or to stop the Investiture or to kill Charles or any other members of the Royal Family. Targets were carefully selected and meticulous care was taken to ensure that no one was injured.

The strategy of M.A.C.'s campaign was based on the realisation that there is no way to challenge successfully the hegemony of the advanced capitalist state while wearing padded gloves. If one is to gain anything at all then one must threaten the state's authority and do so in a way that attracts sympathy and support. Despite the centrality of constitutional methods of action with regard to societal consensus it is perfectly possible to undertake extraconstitutional action without alienating the population in whose name one acts. (This was demonstrated again in the winter of 1979-80 when people without any connections whatsoever with the nationalist movement, who would never condone the removing of a road-sign or the damaging of a television transmitting station, openly expressed their sympathy with those responsible for the burning of second homes.) With this in mind M.A.C. undertook its campaign which was to play a significant role in getting central government to realise once and for all that nationalism in Wales was a powerful force capable of undermining the British state. (An account of the bombing campaign is to be found in Roy Clews' *To Dream of Freedom*.)

It would be said by many that the bombing achieved nothing in terms of concrete conscessions and that it failed to prevent the fiasco of the Investiture. But that was never the aim, and whether one likes it or not, the bombing, like the burning of second homes, succeeded in its aim of raising Welsh consciousness and to this day influences Government policy. Were it not for its fear of precipitating further violence by permitting Gwynfor Evans to die it is doubtful whether the Government would have changed its plans for the Fourth Channel in Wales. Violence is a part of the objective reality of Welsh politics and will remain so until such time as the conditions responsible for its emergence are removed.

Following his arrest and questioning by police, John Jenkins was held on remand at Shrewsbury and Risley prisons until his trial in April 1970. The next twenty months he spent in H.M.P. Winson Green, Birmingham and in London's Wormwood Scrubs from where the first letters in this collection were written. Then on the 1st of January, 1972 he was 'ghosted', as prison jargon has it, to Albany Prison on the Isle of Wight where he was to spend the remainder of his sentence, with the exception of one month spent at Bristol Prison to receive accumulated visits.

Throughout the duration of his sentence Jenkins was a model prisoner: he sang in the prison choir, was awarded prizes for art-work, completed an Open University course and was awarded a degree in Social Sciences. He lost only one week's remission (time deducted from sentence in lieu of good behaviour) and that, three weeks before his release, for having taken part in an all-prison strike. Other than that his behaviour was exemplary.

However, contrary to what one might expect, his good behaviour had little bearing on the way he was treated by the authorities. In theory the categorization of prisoners is to some extent intended to reflect their conduct and although it was natural enough for Jenkins to enter prison as a Category 'A' prisoner he remained on the 'A' List until mid-1975. This led to his mail being delayed for as long as three months —letters would often be sent to the Home Office for censoring rather than to the prison censor. When he complained and asked why this was so, he was told, "Because your name is John Jenkins".

He encountered similar difficulty with visits. Long-term prisoners are entitled to one hour's visit per three weeks but in the case of Category 'A' prisoners, visits must be approved by the Home Office and prospective visitors vetted. This some-times includes visits by local police to the homes of prospective visitors. What exactly is supposed to be achieved by such visits is not known, but one can be sure that it is not the duty of police officers conducting visits actively to discourage people from visiting a prisoner as happened in the case of more than one of John Jenkins' visitors.

An excellent example of Home Office paranoia concerning the 'type' of people allowed to visit Jenkins is mentioned in a letter of September 1972. Earlier that year Jenkins had divorced his wife and became responsible for the education of his two sons, Vaughan and Rhodri. To this purpose he requested a visit from one of their teachers, Mrs Eileen Beasley, a member of the Welsh Department at Ysgol Gyfun Rhydfelen. The request was turned down as were many others and as a result the total number of people allowed to visit Jenkins during his imprisonment was considerably limited.

Such pointless intimidation failed to break John Jenkins' spirit. As the reader can see for himself Jenkins retained his sanity, his political perception and his sense of humour —no easy task when serving a ten-year sentence.

Release from prison and returning to normal conditions is never an easy process, especially so, after a long period of imprisonment in a maximum-security prison. However John Jenkins' return to Wales was made infinitely more difficult than usual. Following his release he was destined to permanent surveillance by the Special Branch who to this day take a never-ceasing interest in his affairs.

The plans to establish a fishing co-operative in Pembrokeshire discussed in some of the letters came to nothing due to lack of financial support. Each of the project's potential sponsors had died by the time Jenkins was released. Having spent some time looking for employment in September 1977 he was appointed to the post of community organiser at the South Wales Anti-Poverty Action Centre (S.W.A.P.A.C.) at Merthyr Tudful, but any hopes he had of a peaceful future were soon dashed. In 1979, an interview recorded with reporter Sulwyn Thomas for BBC Wales' Welsh-language magazine programme *Heddiw* was banned by the BBC and public attention focussed on the man and his ideas yet again. A transcript of the interview was subsequently published in *Y Faner*, a weekly Welsh-language magazine, and it is indeed difficult to understand why the BBC decided to ban the broadcast. Perhaps it had something to do with the Special Branch officers who, from a distance, observed the mountain-top filming of the interview. The controversy surrounding the incident was however mild in comparison with what was to follow.

On December the 13th, 1979 four holiday homes on the west coast of Wales were gutted by fire and by April the 28th the number of arson attacks on holiday homes had reached thirty-seven. Although no authenticated statement accepting responsibility was ever recieved from any organisation and no one has yet been charged with what the police regard as the genuinely politically-motivated burnings it does not require more than a modicum of common sense and political acumen to realise that the burning of second homes was a carefully planned and well-implemented campaign; the first overtly violent campaign of its kind since the bombing campaign of the sixties.

John Jenkins was immediately singled out by the police as a prime suspect and the droves of London-based journalists who now flocked to Wales did their utmost to discover a link between Jenkins and the fires. He was, of course, questioned by police and subsequently released without charge and appeared on a controversial film-report broadcast on BBC TV's *Nationwide* programme. As in other interviews given to television or newspaper reporters John Jenkins was perfectly candid when answering questions concerning his political views. He does not repent in any way for his past actions but since the fact that he is now known to the authorities precludes him from being involved in any covert campaigns he accepts that he must confine himself to other methods. In many ways his work with S.W.A.P.A.C. has the same aim as his earlier activities —namely increasing people's political awareness and encouraging them to utilise the power at their disposal. The interview attracted a great deal of attention, but would not perhaps be of such importance were it not for the fact that it coincided with John Jenkins' application to follow a course in one of the constituent colleges of the University of Wales —an institution not renowned for its fair-treatment of nationalists.

On the basis of his degree in Social Sciences obtained while in prison and his three years experience with S.W.A.P.A.C. John Jenkins applied, in October 1979, to follow a one-year Social and Community Work Course in the Department of Social Policy and Social Work at University College Swansea. When interviewed by members of the department in February 1980 he volunteered information about his past and was told that it would not affect his application and was led to believe that he had in fact been accepted. The College had previously admitted former Angry Brigade member Hilary Creek following her release from prison after serving a ten-year sentence for her part in a bombing campaign.

However, contrary to what he had been told at the time, he recieved no confirmation or denial of his acceptance for five weeks after the interview. When he telephoned the Department he was informed that "there had been a slight problem of a bureaucratic nature". The following morning he received a letter from the Registry informing him that he was not to be accepted as a student. No reason was given for this refusal.

Acting on Jenkins' behalf, Emeritus Professor J.Gwyn Griffiths of the Department of Classics and Ancient History, contacted Professor Broady, the head of the Department of Social Policy and Social Work, and was told that having interviewed John Jenkins, the Department had decided to offer him a place, but that their decision had been vetoed by and ad-hoc committee called by the Principal, Professor Robert Steele. (A holiday cottage belonging to Professor Steele in the village of Rhyd, near Porthmadog, was one of seven holiday homes occupied by members of Cymdeithas yr Iaith Gymraeg in December 1975.) What exactly was said at the meeting is not known but Professor Broady told Professor Griffiths that he understood that the feeling of the Committee was that the acceptance of John Jenkins would be a 'risk' to the College and it would harm the 'public image' of the College. He also mentioned a suspicion that Jenkins was involved in arson attacks on holiday homes.

Despite repeated requests from prominent Welsh academics, Professor John Griffith of the National Council for Academic Freedom and Democracy, the Student's Union at University College Swansea, the National Union of Students in Wales, Trade Unions and Members of Parliament the College authorities have refused to give any reasons for the rejection of John Jenkins' application. In the face of such silence one can only conclude that he is being refused admission on the grounds of his political beliefs. If that is so, then the College is quite clearly in breach of its Charter which forbids discrimination on religious, political or racial grounds. At the time of writing the campaign to secure a place for John Jenkins continues but the authorities appear adamant in their resolve to maintain their silence and prevent him from acquiring the qualifications to which he is undeniably entitled.

Contrary to the image projected by the authorities and so often reproduced by the media, John Jenkins, as anyone who has met him would know, is a quiet and unassuming man. He is feared by the establishment on account of the fact that he is intelligent, perceptive, and eloquent, but more importantly perhaps because he possesses that quality most feared by authority in its adversaries, namely charisma. By nature he is not a man who attempts to draw attention to himself. His public statements are few and far between and invariably made at the request of journalists and interviewers. The idea of publishing a selection of his prison letters was not his but is, as the reader will surely agree when he has read the letters, a valuable and stimulating exercise.

Rather than select only the most interesting passages and string them together it was decided to preserve the form of the letters and with very few exceptions they are reproduced verbatim. Footnotes have been added mainly for the benefit of those not familiar with Welsh politics in the late sixties and early seventies, and for those who do not understand Welsh a brief glossary is included.

This collection is not, and was never intended to be, a definitive, all-inclusive volume but rather a representative select-ion of personal correspondence spanning a perioed of almost six years. Prisoners are allowed to send two letters per week, one given them by the prison authorities and the other purchased with earnings. Letters are necessarily short and must conform to prison regulations, namely, should not concern conditions within the prison or mention fellow prisoners. Such a collection of letters written over such a period of time necessarily lacks the cohesion and unity of a single work written over a long period of time and re-read and ammended by the author. If the reader expects analytical essays on Welsh politics then he will be disappointed, for what follows is a collection of personal letters which provide the reader with a glimpse of the thoughts of the author over a period of time. The topics discussed include the worries and problems encountered by someone serving a long prison senctence; the art work and Open University degree course undertaken by John Jenkins during the period of his imprisonment; the motives for the action which led to his imprisonment; and explication and evaluation of M.A.C.'s campaign; remarks on Welsh political life during the period of his imprisonment and his hopes and fears for the future. Not only do they provide the reader with an unique insight into the thought of John Jenkins but also with a perceptive commentary on Welsh politics which is often as relevant to the contemporary struggle as it is to the events of the late sixties.

Hoffwn ddiolch i bawb a'm cynorthwyodd gyda'r gwaith o olygu'r llythyrau a pharatoi'r rhagair. Hoffwn ddiolch i Sara Erskine Thomas am gasglu'r llythyrau ynghyd ac am ei chyngor amrhisiadwy; i Ned Thomas am ganiatad i gynnwys y ddau lythyr a gyhoeddwyd yn Planet; *i Dafydd Williams am ganiatad i archwilio hen rifynnau o'r* Welsh Nation; *i Robat Gruffudd am y cyfle i wneud y gwaith ac iddo ef a staff Y Lolfa am eu hamynedd a'u gwaith graenus. Yn olaf, hoffwn ddiolch i John am ei ganiatad parod a'i amser prin. Roedd darllen y llythyrau yn brofiad cyffrous ac 'rwyf ond yn gobeithio y bydd i ddarllenwyr y gyfrol rannu'r un profiad.*

RHODRI WILLIAMS

Ystum Taf
Chwefror 1981

GLOSSARY

M.A.C.: Mudiad Amddiffyn Cymru (Movement for the Defence of Wales)

Er budd Cymru: For the good of Wales

Er mwyn Cymru: For the sake of Wales

Annwyl: Dear

Y werin: The people; the working class of Wales

Cymro Cymraeg: Welsh-speaking Welshman

Saesneg: The English language

Yr iaith: The language; the Welsh language

Cymdeithas yr Iaith Gymraeg: The Welsh Language Society

Hwyl: Best wishes

Hwyl a Hedd: Best wishes and peace

Sais: Englishman

Annwyl Gyd-wladwr: Dear Compatriot

Saeson: The English (people)

Maes: The field

Caerdydd: Cardiff

Sosialaidd: Socialist

Ware teg: Fair Play

Pobl iach: Healthy people (i.e. politically)

Yr Wyddgrug: Mold

1971

H.M. Prison
Wormwood Scrubs
15 January 1971

To Sara Erskine[1]

Dear Miss Erskine,

Thank you so much for the copy of Planet 3 and your most thoughtful letter, which put the fear of Christ in me. I am extremely grateful for your kindness in offering to let me have Planets 1 & 2 free, but as I have been very fortunate and already possess, I think, three of each perhaps you will forgive me if I decline this time.

What I am really sorry about is that there should be any spares; judging by the quality of these first issues that situation should soon rectify itself.

My position is that I must ask you to help extricate me from an untenable situation, fraught with diplomatic difficulties. Let me explain, Mr Gareth Meils[2] the Cymdeithas man has already taken out a year's subscription on Planet for me as a seasonal gift. There is a charming old Rector of Llŷn who sends me his copy when he has read it. Much as I appreciate Planet, and I assure you I do, I find that one copy is sufficient of each issue. I would be inclined, except for two reasons, to accept the gift from everyone and leave them happy, but you know as well as I, that all the organisations, societies, cults, claques, cliques, parties, movements and conspiracies, contain the same people. Apart from Vera McGregor's bunch, those who count in Wales are those who care, and I can imagine the scene one night when they all meet under some useful guise, and each is informed by everyone else that he has arranged my issue of Planet. Every-

---

[1] **Sara Erskine:** Executive Editor of *Planet* and wife of Ned Thomas.
[2] **Gareth Miles:** Founder-member of Cymdeithas yr Iaith Gymraeg.

body will of course cancel, and I will be left with no issue, and by then I am quite sure you won't have a spare in the place. (It was obvious that Planet was going to be a wild success from the comments on the first issue, praise from the cream of the literati, the Times, the Guardian, the Western Mail, and a bad tempered swing from the handbag of the darling of the castrati himself.)

The second reason is that I am of course destitute, and it would be most useful if Harri Webb[3] could see fit to use the money to get me some more Western Mails. It is a dreadful paper, nothing but a rag, but it has a monopoly so it is essential. My last coppers went on taking out a subscription up to 8 Feb. 71, after that I descend to a passed copy of the Mirror. It is, of course, a local paper but as I am not a native of the Old Kent Road, and am only passing through this area, it has no relevance for me.

I wonder if you could perhaps let Harri Webb know that you have just been checking the books and you find that I am already receiving Planet, and that chats with a mutual friend have established that I could do with the Western Mail. I am very touched that an artist of Harri Webb's stature thinks of me and wishes to help, but having read and enjoyed his works, it is clear that he knows more about my motivation than I do. I would write to him myself, except that I know it is difficult enough to get near the bar in Merthyr as it is, without having to fight one's way through the massed ranks of the Special Branch.

I find it rather ironic that although the police officially estimate that I cost the taxpayer £7 million, I don't have the price of a paper which I don't want and must have. I realise that I am being very cheeky, and that you must be extremely busy, but help me Miss Erskine, and I will send you a letter in code which will ensure that for the rest of your life you will never need to buy another drink. The minute you approach a bar, the Special Branch man will be there at your side, and will give you drink until it runs out of your ears in the hope that you will become more veritas in vino. This is one of the

---

[3]**Harri Webb**: Poet (1920-).

reasons why Wales is full of veritable winos who bless the inspired day they belched my name and winked significantly. They probably still remember the hush that followed, and are still trying to place the friendly strangers who have been as ready to broach casks as subjects ever since. I remember one night in a patriotic pub, one week after the Helsby exploits,[4] meeting a professional Welshman who was able to let us all in on the highly secret details of the operation. Of course, we all bought him pints until he was paralyzed, because we were all so interested, particularly me, as I had carried out the operation.

Please forgive the garrulity, one gets like this after being locked up. I do not anticipate any change of address, Her Majesty does not seem to find my occupation of her bed here unwarranted, but if she decides to send me out of town, I shall of course let you know. Finally, perhaps you could let Harri Webb have the enclosed cutting from an Irish newspaper (I expect you know I am only allowed one letter a week issued and one bought). May I wish Planet through you, the very best of luck. It only needs luck because it has absolutely everything else in abundance.

Er budd Cymru,

J.B. Jenkins

(M.A.C.)

---

[4]**Helsby Exploit:** Successful M.A.C. operation which destroyed water pipelines at Helsby, near Hapsford in Cheshire, Friday June 28th 1968. See *To Dream of Freedom*, Roy Clews: Y Lolfa, 1980.

To Sara Erskine

Dear Miss Erskine,

I hope you and your colleagues are well and waxing fat on your oft-acknowledged financial support from the Welsh Arts Council. I also hope you are all on your knees frequently thanking God that the Tories are in; Peter[1] will let you get away with it because you are witty and glossy, but George[2] would have your guts for garters and the financial support for afters.

Thanks for your letter, and for taking all the trouble on my behalf with Harri Webb; the Wail is coming through regularly even to this outpost of empire. I sat back when I heard that the Planet for Feb/March had arrived, confident in the knowledge that this time there would be one not three, but to my amazement there were two. The following day a letter arrived from Saunders Lewis[3] telling me that he thought I should be introduced to the delights of this new literary publication Planet, so now I have given up. If *He* thinks I need two, then clearly I need two and I am going to lie back and enjoy it if it kills me.

In many ways living here is like being in a mediaeval cloistered monastic hell, but the librarian is very enlightened and therefore any old books, magazines etc. would be most welcome, and very kind of you indeed to offer. On the other hand, stamped-addressed envelopes are very similar to Thompson sub-machine guns; you are allowed to send as many as you wish —but of course I am not allowed to receive them.

I dropped a line to Harri Webb some time ago, but un-

---

[1] **Peter:** Peter Thomas M.P., Conservative Secretary of State for Wales, (1970-74), and John Jenkins' defending counsel at his trial.

[2] **George:** George Thomas M.P., Labour Secretary of State for Wales, (1968-70).

[3] **Saunders Lewis:** Poet, dramatist, literary critic. Founder member of Plaid Cymru whose radio lecture *Tynged yr Iaith* (The Fate of the Language) became the inspiration of Cymdeithas yr Iaith Gymraeg (The Welsh Language Society).

fortunately at the time there was a big sewage works strike in London, and I joked about the possibility of sabotage being responsible for drowning the place under six feet of glug. Some babu or mandarin must have become obsessed with a vision of glug-or-bust Harri leading a legation of lourge lizards from Lampeter to launch the lethal lurgies on London. Anyway my letter didn't get through; obviously someone thought it would create a big stink.

A few weeks after I was convicted last year, the babus of Llanishen caught up with me, and I found myself in receipt of a tax form asking me what I expected my earnings to be in 1970/71. I wrote back and mentioned that on the night of the France/Wales rugger international 1968, in case no-one had noticed, the Post War Credit files buildings[4] disappeared, and for those who had noticed, was no doubt still sadly missed. I then informed them that in fact I had arranged its demolition, as a result of which I was being kept where H.R.H. could keep a probably drunken, certainly jaundiced eye on me for years. I then followed through with a swift demand for a rebate for 1969, and got it the following week. Which goes to prove that honesty is the best policy, but by Christ there must be an easier way to get some service round here.

People keep saying that the M.A.C. is against the heir to the English throne, but in fact it tried hard to give him the opportunity to prove that what certain people said was true and that he was truly the Messiah. The moment should have occurred the day after the Investiture when he could have been observed (had all gone well) walking on the water to get from the Britannia to Llandudno. Unfortunately, it appears that the very large bomb designed to blow Llandudno pier back to Lancashire, did not go off as planned, so he was able to use it. I don't suppose his advisers have yet seen fit to let him and the public know that he must have been within 5-10 feet of certain death as he stepped on the pier —certainly within hours of the bomb failing to explode, I am told, and the police have confirmed that phone calls were made in spite of which they claim that

---

[4]Post War Credit files buildings: Destroyed by M.A.C. bomb, 5th March, 1968. See *To Dream of Freedom*, Chap. 19.

nothing was found (although an explosives dog was most inter-ested in one particular area). But, naturally, as 'Private Eye' would say, the fact that this episode has never been publicly revealed has absolutely nothing to do with Chief Supt. Jock Wilson of the Special Branch, being promoted to Commander for taking such good care of Armstrong-Jones' dear nephew, over the period of the Investiture and following tour.

As an encore and a finale, I had arranged to get rid of Big Ben in the hope that the concussion would bring the house down, and possibly even get the cabal out of their armchairs at White's, but alas, I was rudely interrupted, and I do not suppose I will ever be allowed to get back to that particular drawing board.

Thank you again for your friendly support, Miss Erskine, and your great kindness, and the potential of your patronage later. I would be grateful for a postcard view of Llangeitho letting me know when you received this letter, so that I can work out first class times and distances.

Er mwyn Cymru,
J.B.Jenkins (M.A.C.)

To Cyril Hodges[1]

Annwyl Mr Hodges,

I hope that you and your family? are well and I thank you for your most welcome and thought-provoking letter. Please forgive the brevity, but I am limited to the confine of this letter, so I will press on forthwith. I am pleased at last to enter into a dialogue with one of your viewpoint, and what strikes me is that our conceptions of objective are as different as our strategy. Your objective is an autonomous Wales while mine is an autonomous Cymru Gymraeg; your enemy is therefore apathy and mine is time, and by that token you can afford to wait while I cannot. Culture is not a land or a country, it is the people, and the graphs are telling a terrible story, so because I want more I must risk more.

This is why I am unable to comprehend your being perfectly reconciled to the fact that you may never see Wales a free country again; for the free Wales which will eventually emerge without fierce and ruthless forcing, will not be a Wales we will know or want to know. History has proved that beyond a certain point the rot cannot be stopped, and at the rate our monoglot Welsh speakers are dying and our young ones leaving and being neutralised by the mass media, the minimum number which will provide a secure foundation for our Welsh State is being approached too quickly. My argument rests on the fact that we are nearing the deadline too rapidly to be reconciled by the too-slow note of potential succour.

I detect the fact that our basic understanding of politics seems to differ, particularly regarding the functions of the State. The first duty of the State is to maintain the integrity of its external borders and to secure Law & Order internally; to this law all else is subject and in an emergency all countries assume the right to suspend Democracy, Christianity, and

---

[1]Cyril Hodges: Poet (1915-74). Not known to John Jenkins before his imprisonment and the two never met since Cyril Hodges died while John Jenkins was in prison.

indeed anything they feel inhibiting to this fight for survival. I do not express approval of this policy, but its existence is a political factor of the first importance, and in fact the tightrope bridging the gap between the pragmatism and morality of state affairs should be walked on only by experts who are aware of the rules. These rules are simple —if you fall off you have failed.

You mentioned the tragedy of Bangla Desh and most aptly, because this epitomises the difference between our views. You clearly believe that Yahya Khan is the villain of the piece, because he sent an Army into B.D. and 'murdered them wholesale'. Naturally, I deplore his activities, but it must be said that he acted in the way expected of any Head of State on the occasion of a potential split in the State. He simply cannot accept the loss of power and property, democratically voted for or otherwise. The true villain is in fact the Sheik of B.D. for occupying a high political position and yet being completely naïve of the realities of power, and, therefore proving a poor shepherd to his flock. He obviously believed that just because he had a large majority behind him, and was being democratic and correct, that he was in an impregnable moral position; and indeed, so he was, except that what was on issue was not a ruling on morality, but a request for the transfer of political power. This request meant the potential fragmenting of Pakistan, and therefore the law of survival was implemented by Yahya Khan acting on the duty of the State. Had the Sheik of B.D. been a politician instead of a moral leader he should have realised all this and acted accordingly. I am a simple Welsh peasant, but even I realise that he should have quietly, over the preceding months, built up an army, an alliance with a neighbouring state regarding help and the denial of air space to West Pakistan, a good intelligence service, and planted men in sensitive areas of the Western Capitals to assure all on the day that the corruption of Yahya's regime was leading to Communism. Then, one dark night he could have moved his forces into position on the borders, and the following day presented Yahya with his arguments for devolution, the moral reasons for the secession and the military reasons why Yahya should accept them. The law of survival would then have localised itself on West Pakistan and militated against any move on B.D. What the Sheik should have done therefore was dirty, underhanded, sly, immoral and necessary. It would have resulted in his being revered as a leader of foresight and courage, saved many thousands of his people from slaughter and established a secure Bangla Desh. I deplore the whole thing whichever way it turned out, it sickens one brought up on the Bible, but one *must* acknowledge these things as fact of life. When cleaning the Augean stables, one must expect to become spattered with manure.

My fight was in fact intended to complement yours. It was not to win Wales by violence, but to use violence as the only means available, with regard to the time left and the conditions obtaining, to awaken the national consciousness and thereby lay the foundations for your majority rule. You need not convince me of the need for constitutional action. I believe in it and I would like to use it, but when 'they' monopolise the mass media, how else but by drama can one get the headlines, and thereby cause thousands of hitherto ignorant people to say "What's all that in aid of?" and be told.

Finally, you say that perhaps you are mistaken or perhaps I am. I would ask you to remember that if I am wrong I risk only my life, but if you are wrong you risk Wales itself. When you go to England you are not simply asking for your rights, and there is no point in quoting from the Bible. You are going there to ask for a transfer of Political pwer, and if you get it you will be making history —World History.

It is analogous to a medical missionary going out to start a Leper Colony. He sincerely believes in God and he accepts that God is capable of performing the miracle of removing Leprosy at any time. This knowledge and belief however does not inhibit his building a hospital to do what he can, in case God may not decide to perform the miracle in this lifetime if at all. I must therefore ask you to understand my lack of reliance on miracles. I prefer to accept the inevitablilities provided time and again by History, and to accept as a miracle the fact that we as Welsh people are here at all —we can expect no more. We therefore owe it to our unborn generations to ensure their survival and I feel we must use any and all means compatible with the basic law of survival to achieve this end. Mr Hodges, I assure you that if you can prove me wrong, I will be absolutely delighted and relieved.

Er mwyn Cymru,
J.B.Jenkins (M.A.C.)

To Audrey White[1]

Annwyl Mrs White,

Many thanks indeed for your most welcome and refreshing letter, received, I fear, some time ago, but I am sure you understand that we are unable to answer letters here at will.

I say, and, reapeat, "welcome" and "refreshing" not for my sake alone, but for the sake of our old Mother Wales, who will need to start really worrying when letters like yours cease to be written. I do not personify our country because of a sentimental streak, although I am not glacial and iron-hard normally, but because it is the best way to describe her in relation to my personal feelings.

She is not a beautiful young girl after whom I lust, or an old duchess whose money and status I desire; she is old, well past her best, decrepit, boozy, and has taken strange bedfellows without the saving grace of desperation. From the material side, she has nothing to give me, in fact by denying her I could better myself by securing an enromous mess of pottage.

I owe her my love and my loyalty, she is my mother. She may be a liability but is the sort of liability that a crippled child is, in the eyes of its parents. If I ignore her in her hour of need no one will ever know or condemn, except myself, and I have the sort of conscience that stops functioning the moment I stop breathing.

I "took up arms" because with many other people, I could feel instinctively that our national identity, our sacred soul, our everything, was not only being threatened but was in the last stages of survival. My aim was to create a state of mind, so that people would not accept all that the English Government said and did as Moses on the Mount; to make them realise that all acions are acceptable when performed in the national interest. I am afraid that I must be a heretic now in what I am about to say, but I do not see the light in Plaid Cymru's tunnel. The

---

[1] The text of this letter and of the next is reproduced from *Planet* 5/6 Summer 1971. The exact dates of writing are not known.

party's leaders are possessed of a strange logic very similar to the English one which believes fully in Independence for every one except Wales. They send messages of solidarity to Makarios, questions are asked in the House about the Basques, they write articles about the Bretons, and the people of Catalonia; but they have delighted the Establishment by refusing to mention me or what I stood for in the Nationalist press, the only hope I ever had of allowing the people to see my side. Let us agree that if something does not happen soon the Wales we know will vanish, the Wales we wish will never be. At least the only price of my ideals is the loss of my freedom; the leaders of Plaid Cymru are prepared to accept the loss of Wales itself as the price for their respectability. They seem to believe that because what they want is right and what their opponents want is wrong, that they will automatically get it. I would suggest that they put the Bible down and study their history books, particularly the British Empire parts. Even their Biblical knowledge is very biased and partisan —had they made rather less of Job, then I would have not have had to make more of David.

It would seem that whereas opium has become the opiate of England, the opiate of Wales is the leaders of Plaid Cymru. My firm belief is that a Wlaes made free by their "normal channels" —constitutional methods, may be free but will certainly be Saesneg. My friends lost their lives, I and others have lost our freedom for a Wales, free and Cymraeg, and I will never settle for anything less. The fight is not only against inertia and apathy but against time itself, because Cymraeg can only be saved and a cultural renaissance created by an Independent Welsh Government, and, if, by the time such a Government exists, the proportion of Welsh speakers has reached a certain level, then as the Irish have found out, there is nothing that can be done to save it, or it can only hope for an expensive and artificial prolongation, divorced from the main daily culture of the people.

We must always remember that to be liked is fatal, because all we can hope for then is benign toleration. We must aim preferably at being hated, then at least we will gain a healthy respect. Remember that the tender approach of the authorities over the

Dulas and Senni, is *not* a direct result of the leaders of Plaid Cymru and the deacons signing hymns in the streets of Liverpool.

Force is to diplomacy what bullion is to banknotes. I have always believed that there is a direct connection between one's social attitude towards a people, and its fighting record.

I hope you and your husband have not gained the impression that I am a blood thirsty militarist. It is simply that the Government has placed us in the final position where we either become men or mice; there is no honourable position in between.

Thank you again for your interest, so essential to one in prison. Incidentally, perhaps you would let me have your professional opinion of my son's spoken Welsh.

My regards to your husband.

> Er mwyn Cymru,
> J.B.Jenkins (M.A.C.)

To Gwyn Williams

Annwyl Mr Williams,

It is extremely heartening to know that there are some people who understand what I was trying to do and why it was, and is necessary. Yet there are still those who believe that I was waging a physical war to achieve some sort of military victory, that in fact I intended among other things to deny water to the English conurbations. As people who understand these things, like yourself, now know, the strategy was military, to achieve a short term mental attitude leading to a long term political settlement. The fight was not to stop water but to create a state of mind; the blowing up of the water-pipes was strategy. I will not consider even the first phase of the struggle, a success, until there is a constant stream of patriots filling up the prisons. The one sure sign of bad government is the steady depopulation, and the one sure sign of a real resurgence is a never ending stream of patriots prepared to be nailed on the cross of conscience.

I am paying heavily, but I will be able to look my grand-children in the eyes when they ask the question that the likes of George Thomas will be unable to answer. "And when Wales was being destroyed in the sixties and seventies where were you, and why didn't you stop it."

The people of Wales need not worry that I came along —they must really start worrying when the flow stops.

Of course it can be said that violence is unnecessary and that Plaid Cymru have the answer. To this I would agree; there is no doubt that Wales will inevitably become independent. My proviso is that by the time independence arrives the Wales we know and hate/love even now will have long gone; the Wales we wanted Free and Welsh will be absolutely unattainable.

The Cymdeithas yr Iaith Gymraeg is fighting a good fight, but even if they win every round, they will lose at the final bell. Ireland has proved that even when the Government is eagerly in support of a culture and language, that is not enough. One cannot deal with a culture in isolation because it is an integral part of life, and by life I mean economics and politics. Let us take Blaenau Ffestiniog; there the Government has announced that it will do (and has done) much for the language. But if they subsidise the chapels, the schools, and have a Gymanfa every night, it will have no lasting effect. The people will leave because the old industries are running down; new firms will not come because the roads are not good and the area is out of the main stream for the main centres of distribution. Therefore a political decision (which could only be implemented by a Welsh Government) would have to be made involving economic consequences – the culture would then take care of itself.

Let me now discuss the last part of your letter where you accuse the English of hypocrisy and double-dealing. As far as the English are concerned the difference (and there *is* a difference) between the Nationalist Fanatic and the dedicated partiot is this – the Dedicated Patriot is the brave man who fights his way on to the beaches and up to the heights of the mineral rich foreign land, and plants the Union Jack in a sea of blood. The people who try to stop him and who provide the blood are the nationalist fanatic. Realistically speaking, it doesn't really matter what you do, why you do it or even how you do it. What matters is for whom you do it. When the Germans had occupied Jugoslavia, Churchill sent arms to Tito rather than Mikaelovic (for the Christian reason that he had killed more Germans) and announced that Tito by virtue of his acts had "saved the soul of Jugoslavia". History is full of these acts but amid all the left hand/right hand dealing, the throat cutting/back biting, one thing stands firm and fast as the Rock of Gibraltar. England's actions when weighed with the tenets of Christianity and the Bible more often than not were foul and indefensible, but of course England did not use the criteria of Christ, but the dogmatic realism of the national interest. This same national interest is as much my right as theirs and they do not have a monopoly of the right to determine the national interest of Wales.

At least, all that I was prepared to sacrifice was my life and my freedom for my ideals. I oppose the leaders of Plaid Cymru because they are prepared to sacrifice their people, their country and their heritage, on the shrine of their respectability and pacifism.

My best wishes,
Er mwyn Cymru,
J.B.Jenkins (M.A.C.)

To Cyril Hodges

Annwyl Mr Hodges,

Many thanks for your two thought-provoking letters; it is very good of you to go to all the trouble and bother of typing them out. May I say that I am sincerely sorry to hear of your illness, and that I hope you have learned to adjust to your limitations in order to be able to give people, like myself, the benefit of your observations. Your name rings a bell, I expect it is too much of a long shot, but some months ago I remember reading a most touching and beautiful epitaph to Gwenallt[1] in 'Sobornost'.[2] I distinctly recollect the reflection that Gwenallt must have been a wonderful person to have inspired such an eulogy, and I am almost sure the author was a Hodges.

Thank you for your remarks on the letters in 'Planet'. I can only assure you that I had no inkling the letters would be published, and the first I knew of it was when they were staring me in the face out of 'Planet'. I only hope they will not be regarded as a wet blanket by Cymdeithas yr Iaith and as a denunciation by the Blaid. I intended them to show the C.yr I. that a cultural struggle alone is not enough, but must be encouraged and actively aided by a strong political leadership; and as a reasoned plea to the Blaid to face realities and to adjust itself to the final make-or-break crisis of our nation.

The biggest threat to Wales is an internal one and is provided by extremists and nationalists acting together. I refer of course to the many active English nationalists in Wales (who are by blood and birth Welsh) and to the many extreme pacifists who assist them by not opposing them.

I have no illusions about my position in the general scheme of things; I was not down in the cellars shaking the foundations, but was the crack in the wall. People have said that what I did gave Wales a bad name and was bad for Plaid Cymru; my

[1]**Gwenallt:** D.Gwenallt Jones, Poet, (1899-1968).

[2]**Sobornost:** The Journal of the Fellowship of St. Alban and St. Sergius. See: Series 6 No. 1 summer 1970 'Gwenallt' by H.A.Hodges (sic).

answer to that is that I was not interested in the good name of Wales, but in the survival at all costs of Holy Wales (not necessarily to be confused with pacifist Wales). As to the P. Cymru complaint: before the campaign started, Gwynfor Evans came to Wrexham and addressed a well-publicised meeting — about 30-40 turned up. After my betrayal and capture and trial, there was an enormous uproar in all the North Wales and local papers, and when Gwynfor Evans appeared again at a meeting after my conviction, the entire hall was packed out to the doors.

Your assumption that Ned Thomas of 'Planet' was the the only editor with sufficient integrity to publish my letters, is in fact wrong, and the explanation illustrates the position Plaid Cymru places us in by her ignoring of our claim to be heard. Audrey White mentioned to me on her visit here in May that Gwilym Jones of 'Y Faner' had published excerpts —in Welsh, after translation by Audrey. Naturally the W. Mail & Liverpool Daily Post would never dram of publishing, *and neither would the Welsh Nation* for the reasons I have mentioned of extremism & nationalism.

You should not really denigrate fanaticism as such; perhaps if you regard the matter as one of semantics and think of it as an obsession with an ideal, or a deeply dedicated sense of purpose, or even an unswerving objectivity, it will not cause such fear . I will say three things about fanaticism: firstly that if it is true that a fanatic has the strength and drive of ten men, it is necessary because the other nine can't be bothered. Secondly it is not always true that a fanatic doesn't count the cost of taking action; I became a fanatic because I was not prepared to accept the result of inaction. Lastly, if Wales is to survive and her culture and heritage flourish, it will be done only by the ferocious and unswerving devotion to Wales above all else. "All else" includes family, prospects, careers, health, freedom & life itself. I believe, in fact, I *know* that Wales *can* inspire this sort of fanaticism, and that this fanaticism is the essential catalyst required to move the majority of the people.

I wonder if you would do me a favour, Mr Hodges. You are not allowed to send me S.A.E. or send money for that purpose.

I am allowed one letter per week and one extra which I buy, and this means I have to do two jobs at times with one letter. Would you place me in your debt by forwarding this bill to Audrey White for honouring as soon as she possibly can, please. Audrey & Gwyn Williams (and Albert of course) control the public fund for my family; I asked Gwyn one month ago to see to the bill, but from what I gather the letter did not get to him, and my wife has received a 'final' one which makes the matter urgent. Talking of Anglo-Welsh magazines, have you ever tried 'Poetry Wales' from Chris Davies. I can thoroughly recommend it.

Er mwyn Cymru,
J.B.Jenkins (M.A.C.)

H.M.Prison
Wormwood Scrubs
4 September 1971

To Sara Erskine

Annwyl Sara,

I hope you, Ned, children and friends are well, happy, and rested after your holiday.

I am most grateful for the two 'Cancer Ward' books which I am thoroughly enjoying. Ned's book, I have not read, —I have eaten again and again and each time I am more amazed at his complete insight. It is so powerful and factual that I am surprised at the Mule[1] even bringing itself to mention it, let alone review it.

All men are composed of reason and emotion and instinct in greater or lesser proportions. Had I been one of those driven almost entirely by the latter qualities, the book would have explained my motivation to me and it would have been as a revelation: as it is, my reason confirms the utter correctness of Ned's logic, the definitiveness of the book as a study, and the potential of Ned as a dangerous catalyst to the emotions of the werin. The book will be seen by some as a tolling of bells at a graveside and will be read through a haze of tears; others will see it as a call to arms and will read it through the red eyes of order and the salt sweat of murder. But it cannot be ignored, and if I am to end as a shadow against a wall, I wish the shadow to be that of a Cymro Cymraeg.

There were just two factors, which although not entirely missed, could have done with a little mor detail, and the one was linked with the other. I refer to the fact that the two men who died were English-speaking only, and that although Welsh-speaking Welshmen feel threatened, there is a significant body of English-speaking Welshmen who feel equally for the language, and in fact possess an added dimension, in the bitterness due to deprivation. I realise that Ned could not have known of this, because only lately, thanks to his own efforts, have any of·these feelings been publicised. There has been a

[1] **the Mule**: The *Western Mail*, the South Wales daily newspaper owned by the Thomson Group.

series of carefully calculated wedges driven between the Cymraeg and Saesneg Cymro by the activities of the State officials and their toadies; these wedges have taken the form of an accentuation of differences, and a total suppression of the bridges between the groups, namely people like myself. Plaid Cymru with its usual attitude has naturally assisted the State, and has thereby helped some of us to believe that the only effective democratic and constitutional way of redress is to place certain people up against a democratic wall and convert them with constitutuional machine-guns.

I was saddened to read your assessment of the Selene people in which you imply that they are weak-willed nomads who find people difficult. I feel they are analogous to the Hippo Birds who think they are eagles but belong with the pigs. At least they prove it is possible to make a pig's ear out of a silk purse. I do certainly agree with you that there is room for negative protest, as long as it is understood that there is a time limit, after which the activists will proceed to activate the inactive. It is too much to expect them to compliment me, but I would like them to admit that I complement them and then we could complement each other effectively.

*　　　*　　　*

My regards and tell Ned to keep stoking up the Welsh way of strife until Wales becomes a land fit for heroes to die in.

Er mwyn Cymru,
John (M.A.C.)

To Cyril Hodges

Annwyl Cyril,

I hope that this letter finds you in good health and heart.

Firstly, let me thank you most sincerely for the Welsh Course which arrived here in my cell today. It is clear that your taste is impeccable, and if I am unable to advance myself in yr Iaith then it must be my own fault, because the instructions are lucid.

How very lucky I am to be able to count you among my good friends, and how very helpful your letters have proved to be. I have recently been undergoing a personal crisis, during which I was grateful beyond measure for any indication that there was anyone outside these walls who was aware of my existance. Your letters continued to arrive, and your usual lucidity and logical arguments assisted me greatly, thus helping me to arrive at the conclusion that although no one is indispensable —you are.

I am intrigued by your statement that you lived in the hills near Ystrad Mynach, because I also spent the greater part of my life there. I lived in Penybryn, where my parents are still and my one brother is at Gellygaer, so I am very curious as to the whereabouts of your early residence, because I am bound to know it well.

I was about to say that I am unable to account for my rather atypical Nationalist feelings, for that area, which has never been particularly noted regarding its extreme political figures. Then I remembered that in 1965-66, I visited the leading light of the Capel Cymraeg (Horeb —at Gelligaer) to ask him to bring some support for the establishment of an Ysgol Gymraeg for Gelligaer into his columns, as he was the Merthyr Express correspondent for the area. As there was no school there (and there *still* isn't to my deep disgust) I suggested that instead of complaining of the falling adult membership of his chapel, and the lack of linguistically qualified youth coming forward, he would at least ensure the survival of his chapel by a little discreet assistance.

To my utter amazement, he immediately jumped to his feet and wanted to know whether this suggestion of mine had emanated from Plaid Cymru, and if so he wanted nothing to do with it. Nothing I could say or do would persuade him that from the religious, cultural and indeed social point of view, a Welsh School would be an undoubted asset to the area in every way. I realised that this man, although a Cymro Cymraeg, was blind, deaf and dumb, and that his incredible capacity for faith had placed him in the position where he was perfectly prepared to cut off his nose to spite his face. I would have been quite prepared to let him, except that I had to rely on his sense of smell. Meeting, and being rebuffed by, this man, who boasted of the fact that his parents had come from a hamlet in North Wales, was very helpful, informative and fatal to my already forming impressions, because essentially he showed me that if anything was to be done, then I would have to do it. He demonstrated that he was too involved with religion to bother with Welsh Nationalism, and that he was too involved with the Labour Party to bother about culture. I left his house feeling that his God was not Jesus and the Cross, but Janus and the Double-cross. My final word on him is that I made a particular note of the area claimed by him as his birthplace —a little spot called Llanrhaiadr-ym-Mochnant, noted as the area where Bishops translate fervour into words, and where patriots translate bitter yearnings into deeds.

I sometimes feel that had that person devoted the care to human strivings that he had to human failings; that had he modelled his actions on the king of the Jews rather than the Vicar of Bray; then perhaps I would not be here today (but on reflection I would certainly be here tomorrow).

I entirely agree with you about the utter stupidity of Anti-English feeling. I have always maintained that I am not against English rule but rather misrule. I must admit that I consider the chief enemies of Wales as the political prostitutes who thrash around our putrefying body politic with the gusto of big white maggots, and for the same reasons; in order that they might live and grow fat, Wales must decay and die.

Thank you for the offer of a holiday for my sons, but I was so impressed by your letter telling me of my son's demeanour and attitude while with Cynog Davies,[1] that I dashed off a quick letter to Cynog asking if he could do the same again next year. He has not yet replied, so perhaps you would bear with me a little longer. In the meantime, I am appealing to the Commission of Human Rights in Strasbourg, and I was wondering if, having written my appeal out in longhand, you could manage to type it out (my writing, I realise is execrable in the extreme); that is, of course, *if your health permits*. My regards to your wife and yourself.

Er mwyn Cymru
John (M.A.C.)

---

[1] **Cynog Davies:** Founder member of Cymdeithas yr Iaith Gymraeg and author of Society's maniffesto published in 1972. English translation published in *Planet*; 26/27, Winter 1974/75.

To Watcyn Owen

Annwyl Watcyn,

Thank you for your letter, and please forgive my delay, due to the usual reason, for not answering. I am very distressed to hear of your unfortunate state of health, and I hope most sincerely that by this time you will have improved immeasureably. Wales can ill afford to lose any more of her faithful sons, particularly as there are not really all that many left these days.

Thank you for your sympathy regarding my impending divorce; I am reconciled to it by virtue of its inevitability. I am not really bitter about it, because my feelings regarding myself were drained some time ago; anything more is like pouring water on a saturated sponge. After the humiliation of Tryweryn,[1] the agony of Aberfan,[2] the crucifixion of Caernarfon[3] and the attitude of the Blaid to our Welsh dead and imprisoned, I have nothing more to feel with. My one fear is that from the crucible of this prison, heated by the feelings generated by the intense passions I have experienced, what may finally emerge will be something less than human, and may even resemble the "Clever, ruthless, fanatic" I was called at my trial. My worry is that a mind subjected to repeated hammer blows will either retreat within itself and never emerge with any degree of clarity, or will simply for survival's sake, cease to care, and I would prefer to be insane rather than inhuman. What worries me is that I *was* as "hard as steel" as you put it, and what has happened under the fury of the fire is that I am becoming harder. Possibly this is what prison is for, because people, particularly political ones, seem to attach a great deal of

---

[1] **Treweryn:** Valley flooded and used as reservoir by Liverpool Corporation despite unanimous opposition in Wales. After a succession of protests, including bombing of transformer and electricity pylon, the reservoir was finally opened October 21st, 1965.

[2] **Aberfan:** Scene of disaster in October 1966 when coal tip avalanche buried local school killing 144 children, men and women.

[3] **Caernarfon:** Scene of investiture of Charles Windsor as 'Prince of Wales', 1st July, 1969.

importance to it as a school of life.

The one heartening factor is that a few kind people like yourself and Edwina, care enough to keep in touch, and this, especially in prison, helps greatly to prevent the growth of the dehumanising virus which attacks violently and thrives heartily on neglect and loneliness.

What does not help overmuch is when movements display inefficiency to those like myself who have no means of combating it. For instance, Dafydd Williams[4] of H.Q. Plaid Cymru promised faithfully to let me have a copy of "Welsh Nation" while I was in prison. The last one I received was the August edition. Earlier this year I joined the Celtic League and received a letter from Dublin acknowledging my subscription and promising all manner of books etc.; from that day to this I have never received a sign or a gesture from them, and I simply cannot just send them a letter of memory-jogging, because I have the greatest difficulty in keeping in touch with my family and friends due to the shortage of letters.

Anyway to answer your queries. As things are, I have, theoretically, two release dates, one for the first eligibility for Parole, the other for the first release date with remission and good behaviour. The first is June 1973, but can be discounted completely because Category 'A' people are not eligible for Parole; the second is August 1976 which is five years, from now. I have been in prison since 2 Nov. 69, so this is my 3rd prison Christmas coming up; I cannot help but wonder whether the people of Cymru will remember me and the boys who I am sure will also be inside by then.

The other query referred to my being captured. I know the police made a big thing of it, saying that the brilliant work of the Special Branch and the plodding of the C.I.D. together were responsible. In fact I was betrayed, informed on by a woman from the North, who ironically was a Cymraes Gymraeg and a friend, not of mine, but of an acquaintance. What has emerged is that the M.A.C. cost the State £7,000,000, and lost 2 men dead and 2 in prison. My greatest achievement was not the cost to the State, or that they lost so much and saw only two cells

---

[4] **Dafydd Williams:** General Secretary of Plaid Cymru.

destroyed (one by accident and one by betrayal) but that without the informer they never would have broken our cover, and more important, that the complete system of safe houses, dumps, dead letter boxes, active supporters and sleeping sympathisers have to this day completely escaped detection. So, in fact, it is not a matter of waiting for Arthur to wake, but a simler and more efficient and reliable method of reactivating an existing machine which has been proved and has been under fire. However that is an honour which must fall to someone better qualified than myself; I feel that my part has been played and that I should be put out to graze. Thank you Edwina for your letter which was most helpful and not at all "Pious sounding". In turn, I must apologise for getting all technical and revolutionary —it means that this letter will have to filter through a few extra layers of filtration before reaching you eventually. I hope and trust that Watcyn is as well physically as am I by now.

> Er mwyn Cymru,
> John (M.A.C.)

To Cyril Hodges

Annwyl Cyril,

I hope that you and your family are well and happy. For myself, I am undefeated, and this is enough in my circumstances.

Thank you for your recent letters which I am able to answer at last, and I assure you that they remain an essential factor in my decision to remain undefeated.

Of course, I am well acquainted with the area where you used to live. You say that on the sharp bend of the river there is a farmhouse, and in fact an old friend of mine used to live there whom perhaps you knew. He was a nice old Irishman named Dunne, and I believe he was one of two old people who lodged there. I remember in my younger days taking the path past your bungalow, and following the old track to a point near the Golf Course where I would turn right, and end up on the Ystrad — Nelson main road at the house of the manager of Tredomen.

That particular area was the source of much of my inspiration and strength, and my thoughts often wing back there to charge my batteries.

You are commendably modest when you say that you are not in fact a triumphant and respected poet in Wales, but I feel that I must, in this case, insist on my original statement. Firstly, when we began to correspond, I naturally (naturally that is, in view of my background, and I know you will understand) caused enquiries to be made, just in case you could have been a member of the opposition. I will not embarrass you by quoting the reply, but in essence it said that you were very healthy and most talented, and highly respected in literary circles. I have also had the honour of reading some of your work, and more recently have read two reviews of your latest book. The "Welsh Nation" confirmed all I had been told and knew of your literary talent, and the Western Mule by being bitter about your "Xenophobia" more than confirmed your healthy attitude.

Anyone who is praised by the "Nation" and attacked by the "Mule" is just the sort of person Wales needs, and I appreciate.

I think everyone has a secret and sacred place where he is able to commune with his inner self and examine his soul. I have such a place and because you will understand, I propose to describe it to you. At Gelligaer, take the road north to the Cross Inn, then straight on up the mountain to the grid. Go past the old cottage and turn right at the Y junction. Carry straight on, until the road bends sharply to the right. Leave the car and walk about 60 yds to the Celtic cross you will see above the ferns, and you will find yourself at the site of Capel Gwladys, a Chapel of Rest built A.D.450. The site is clearly marked both physically, and for those who understand, mentally also. I always made a point of returning to this spot where I could always be assured of rest, peace, inspiration and solace, and towards the end of the campaign I required much of the latter. I found it most galling that, unlike others with troubled souls, I had no-one in whom to confide, no shoulder on which to lean. The nature of my problems negated the comforting functions normally exercised by a wife or a mother; anyway neither would have understood the burden I bore nor sympathised with me for bearing it.

If you are ever able to get up there, Cyril, go there only on a warm, sunny day. On a dark day the mountain glowers like a black Welsh brow, the bitterness and grief of the ancient and historic area is tangible to anachronistic people, and the rain trickles like the blood that the Romans, Normans and others freely shed in their day. Their day was only yesterday, and even the Romans can be seen for the 'nouveau riche' they were, when regarded in comparison with those who were there before. These were the heartlands of the Silures, and this was the country of Caradoc and the site of the bloodiest defeat suffered by the Normans in the whole of their British campaign. But why should I say these things, Cyril, when you know them already I am sure, and better than I ever will. If you do go to Capel Gwladys ever, and if you are a praying man, perhaps you will be kind enough to mention me. The spirit of the place haunts me and gives me peace even here, and I am grateful.

Thank you for accepting the typing of my petition; as a safeguard perhaps you would hold the original handwritten statement for me, so that I need never worry about losing it in some way. Please forgive the rambling and atypical letter, Cyril I am in one of those strange moods and among strangers, but as a Cymro you will understand. Even fanatics need inspiration and a place to lick their wounds, and I thank God I am a Cymro and have Cymru to love and cherish.

I hope you and your family will enjoy the season of festivity and that your health physically becomes equal to your health mentally. My sincere regards to all.

Er mwyn Cymru,
John (M.A.C.)

H.M.Prison
Albany
30 January 1972

To Miss M.Owen

Dear Sisters,

I salute you with respect and love and I hope that the obvious mental health of yourself and your family is equalled by your physical health.

It is with a deep sincerity that I thank you for the gift you were recently good enough to send to Mr Thomas on my behalf. May I say that your kind gesture reflects the truly Welsh attitude that I respect above all others, and which I believe represents the answer to the barbarian hordes at our cultural and social gates.

Being the people you are, and coming from the cradle of Cymreictod, you will be aware of the reasons which drove me to become a temporary guest of the queen of England. I would like you to know, however, that with the loving sympathy of yourselves and others with me, I am not bitter at my incarceration and that I would do the whole thing again if given a choice.

I thank a kindly fate for my great good fortune in being born a Welshman in this day and age, and for having been given the opportunity to serve the cause of my dear country and beloved people. I welcome my imprisonment and punishment with the open arms of a lover, and I now fully understand for the first time the mystical motivation which sent the early Christians into the arena, and allowed them to serenely sing hymns while being torn to pieces by wild beasts.

On Christmas Eve, I underwent one of the most emotional and intense experiences in my entire life, which convinced me finally of the existence of race memory, instinct and the strong, compelling ties between those who unite in love of country and people. I was sitting down in my little cell, after looking through the bars at the moon shining. The moonlight outside sparkled on the frosty walls and glinted on the menacing tinsel of the barbed wire above them, but I was happy for I was not alone. There were others looking at the same moon who were, like me, in prison for Cymru Rydd a Chymraeg,[1] and others fasting for Christmas, and I was linked to them all in a way unaffected by the walls and wire. At that instant, as I became aware of this, it was as though my thought has completed a circuit which channelled and directed our united love and energy, for I felt a tangible wave of warmth and love flood over and into me. I was completely transformed, my blood was thrilled and singing, and I was possessed by a compelling ecstasy which was pure love for my country and people. I *knew* beyond doubt at that moment, the terrible power of the love which had motivated our fighting ancestors such as Caradoc, Buddug, Arthur, Glyndŵr, Llywelyn; my blood was singing to me of a long race memory of dungeons and death for the cause, and I was so submerged in the compelling ecstasy of sacrifice that I would have welcomed pain with joy. The intensity lasted for perhaps 15 mins. and finally receded slowly leaving me drained but happy and filled with pity for those inadequates who have to resort to drugs for this experience. I knew that I had not been alone, and I knew that we were not going to lose this fight, *because* I had not been alone. All of Wales had been with me in spirit.

Thank you for remembering me, I will keep your letter to help me in moments of doubt.

Live in peace gentle people, with my love and respect.

> Er mwyn Cymru,
> Your brother,
> J.B.Jenkins (M.A.C.)

---

[1]**Others . . . like me in prison for Cymru Rydd a Chymraeg:** A reference to Cymdeithas yr Iaith Gymraeg members who were serving prison sentences at the time.

H.M.Prison
Albany
31 March 1972

To Cyril Hodges

Annwyl gyd-wladwr,

I hope that your family and yourself are well and happy,
Cyril. Thank you for your recent letter, and I am gratified that
you have recovered from your nasty bout of 'flu.

I expect you are wondering why the medieval look at the
beginning of this letter,[1] it is not significant and does not
indicate that my cell is making me monkish, (although I must
admit that I have been in worst places than this for ease of
contemplation). In some ways, the imprisonment of the body
is a good and even necessary discipline, removing as it does, the
usual distractions; one learns, if one didn't know before, how
to sublimate one's basic emotions and urges, into a channel of
strength, which upholds and stiffens one's resolve and will, and
impresses others with one's sincerity by the very intensity of
the emotional force, normally under control but on occasions
bursting through.

I digress because I meant to explain that the curvilinear motif
is an attempt to soften the harsh and functional spartan
impression received by the sight of an official letter. It was also
a chance to be ostentatious with my still precarious nodding
terms regarding yr Iaith.

I am delighted to hear that you are taking up the unfortunate
case of the families in the North; I know that this means an
application of your usual efficiency, which in turn means that
both they and I may rest more easily in our respective prisons.
I must, however, beg you not to tax your strength so soon after
your recent illness; I realise while pressing this, that you are
most unlikely to pay any attention to my urgings, and therefore
I have to add the imperative —for the sake of Cymru.

I feel in my very bones that a time is coming when our

---

[1] **Abergele Martyrs:** Alwyn Jones and George Taylor, the two M.A.C
officials killed whilst planting explosives at Abergele on the 1st of July,
1969.
See: *To Dream of Freedom:* Chapter 29.

people are going to need every ounce of energy and leadership which can be made available. In Cymru there is a great shortage of practical men of stature who are acceptable both in the Boardroom and the Maes, and even rarer circles. You are in an even hotter seat, being an Ambassador between the brains and the heart of the same body. Before I had the pleasure of knowing you well, I believed you to be a business man with an unusual hobby; now, I know you to be a Poet with an unusual occupation.

I find myself in total agreement with you in your analysis of the economic and social position in Cymru, and again in your masterly forecast of the required conditions necessary to right our present fatal evolution. It is a sad fact that many orthodox nationalists believe that running up a flag over Caerdydd City Hall will achieve wonders, and is the culmination of all our hopes and dreams. I believe, with you, that the flag marks the placing of the Welsh foot on the lowest rung of a long ladder; it is the first step in the march of a thousand miles, definite but not by any manner of means, final.

I disagree with you in one single point —where you imply that you are becoming an old man a little too soon, but are assuming the stubborn characteristics of old age even quicker. You are assuming the stubborn characteristics, not of old age, but of an ancient race, and thank God for this most essential of qualities in us. I suppose we are all accustomed by now to the delighted trills which greet any display of English arrogance by the "national" press; yet any action undertaken by a Cymro for survival's sake on behalf of the nation, is described as atavistic and pure anachronistic behaviour, thus demonstrating what we have always known, namely that only an Englishman has a heritage.

Forgive this lame letter, Cyril; I thought I was made of steel, but the domestic events of the last week have shown me that I am still vulnerable to personal pain in response to purely personal stimuli. I am grateful that I had rebuilt my reserves since 1969 so that I find myself withstanding a tendency to emotion over the matter; I still cannot determine whether the pain is a tribute to my humanity or an indictment of the strength of my will. I find it helps to regard it as yet another fire to forge the essential steel in myself, and I firmly believe that my character will be refined as a result. If this is all to the eventual benefit of Cymru, then I am glad but I cannot yet see the wood for the trees.

My regards to your family and for the sake of Cymru take care of your health.

Er mwyn Cymru,
John (M.A.C.)

H.M.Prison
Albany
26 June 1972

To Cyril Hodges

Annwyl Cyril,

I hope that you and your family are well and happy. I also
hope that you are in a particularly forgiving mood with regard
to my shameful neglect of our correspondence. Perhaps it will
help if I assure you that I have written to no-one for one
month; this is the time of year for me to pause and reflect and
to grieve.

Thank you very much for your most kind gift of pens; they
were, of course, very much welcomed. They matched the
originals perfectly (which did not surprise me as they were the
same pens), and I have gained great pleasure from the work I
have since carried out.

To answer your queries; No I do not have that copy of the
"Collected Poems" of Yeats, and yes I have heard "The Green
Desert" by Harri Webb. I am lucky in that I have a record
player which I am allowed to use as an aid to learning Cymraeg
and for any other purpose. My mother sent me the record
which I asked for because you recommended it, and I agree
with you regarding its quality.

I am gratified by the results of the fund set up for the
Abergele martyrs'[1] families. I regard it as a tribute to your
efficiency, but I must disabuse you regarding my "Quixotic
gesture" of sharing the £200. What happened was that a
Cardiff lady contacted Mrs White and told her that she wanted
to give my family the £200. I had already expressed to Mrs
White with some emphasis, my concern over the neglect of our
sisters in the North, so, armed with a knowledge of my feelings
on the matter, she asked the lady if the money could go instead
to them. The lady agreed, and I heard of it when it was already
a fait accompli, from Mrs White on a visit to me here. I was
very pleased both with Mrs White and the lady and endorsed the
action with delight, but the real credit must go to Mrs White
who is an absolute pillar to Cymru and myself.

She has been telling me of various sinister moves made by

those in authority regarding the employment of those known to be free of the slave mind. This ties in with what I have heard from other sources on a Wales-wide basis, dealing with the great difficulty experienced by healthy people in obtaining and keeping employment, particularly those in education. I note with disgust that "they" are at it again in Abergele, this time refusing to allow the Chapel to be used for the Memorial Service.

Presumably had Alwyn and George gone to London, having turned their backs on Cymru, like so many others from that area, and made their money in slum properties and brothels, they would have been buried with full honours like the milk magnates of Ceredigion. Presumably, the Duke of Windsor found favour with these dinosaurs because he turned his back on duty and country to favour his own personal interests. I do not approve of the monarchy or any royalty, regarding them as descendents of the more murderous robber Barons, but I do believe in duty without compromise or expediency. I understand that the Bible lays down "Greater love hath no man but he lays down his life for his friends" but it appears that this only applies when one lays down one's life for the establishment of this consumer society.

George Thomas attacks their actions because he is not blind and can see the threat implied in the long-term objective. The Deacons attack because they are blind and cannot see the promise beyond the short-term tactics.

The real tragedy of the American Indian is not that he was massacred by the legal thugs, or that the legal thugs could say "The only good Indian is a dead one". The real tragedy was that many Indians after being herded on to the reservations and "educated" also came to believe that the only good Indian was a dead one.

There are some things more important than votes and respectability; the Honour and self-respect of our people are some of them. I do not "prefer the bullet and the bomb to the ballot box", any more than I prefer prison or death to freedom or life. But when there is no democratic means of ensuring the survival of a priceless heritage, then I will assume my right to fight for my country. I expect to be vilified by those whom I have to fight, but not by those whose apathy has made my stand necessary. The Church of England backed the wrong horse during the Industrial Revolution, and the Free Churches should pause to ponder at this stage as to where their loyalties lie, or they will go the same way. Is there something shameful about a man dying for his principles, his ideals, or does he set a new standard if his actions are acknowledged? —a standard which must be condemned because it takes guts to emulate it.

My regards Cyril to you and all the family.

Er mwyn Cymru,
John (M.A.C.)

To Cyril Hodges

Annwyl Cyril,[1]

I hope that you and your family are well and happy.

Firstly, many thanks for the most useful felt pens which I appreciate greatly. Secondly, thank you for managing to get to my mother's house; she was very pleased to meet Pegi[2] and yourself, and anything that pleases my parents, pleases me.

Thank you also for your kind remarks on my poor artistic efforts; I am well aware that your ethics as a poet would be as strong as the discipline required by your art, and this knowledge heightens the pleasure I took in your most kind encouragement.

I have since sent you a further five "abstracts" with another about to be despatched; I trust that you received them in one piece.

I write this, Cyril, on the 23rd day of my hunger strike and I feel that I owe it to you to explain that I am not, in fact, "Tamely submitting to intolerable pressures", but making a stand,

[CENSORED]

I was granted custody of my children by a legally appointed Judge in an open court; among my prerogatives is that of the decisive word regarding the education of my sons. My sons' teacher, Mrs Beasley, has expressed her willingness to come here to discuss Vaughan's future, and I feel I must have a professionally trained person who is also personally familiar with, and interested in my son, to advise me on this vital matter. The Home Office has decided that she is not a fit person to visit me, because, "She was not known to me before my imprisonment". Therefore, the position has been reached where the decision of the Judiciary has been set aside by the

---

[1] The gaps left in this letter were left deliberately by John Jenkins who was required by the prison censors to omit certain passages.

[2] Pegi: Mrs Cyril Hodges.

Home Office on a technicality

[CENSORED]

Presumably, I am in prison because I have committed certain offences; it follows that being a "criminal", the people with whom I associated prior to my imprisonment are "criminally"-minded, and therefore my only hope of salvation is to be introduced to people who were unknown to me before imprisonment. This course is forbidden they say, and yet, only last weekend I received a visit from a lady and her husband who *have* been approved by the Home Office, *and whom I did not know before imprisonment.*

[CENSORED]

Again, Cyril, I am not allowed to receive certain political material e.g. Tafod y Ddraig,[3] Cwmni Gwasg Rydd Caerdydd[4] etc., while others are able with impunity to receive all manner of what could be described as disgusting and disgraceful material both pornographic and racist and extreme right wing.

[CENSORED]

conflicts with the Strasbourg convention to which this State is a signatory. I am prepared to bear impossibly heavy burdens, Cyril, but I am unable to

[CENSORED]

then for the pure sake of justice and indeed self-protection, I must seek political status for the benefits. I am not a hardened and toughened criminal, so I want the right to be treated either as a criminal, or a political prisoner; at present I receive the disadvantages of both classes with the benefits of neither. The English State insists that Ulster is as integral a part of the United Kingdom as the Isle of Wight, and in Ulster, men who were convicted like myself, went on hunger strike and as a result have received recognition of their political status with the resultant benefits. I have exactly the same

---

[3] **Tafod y Ddraig:** Monthly magazine of Cymdeithas yr Iaith Gymraeg.

[4] **Cwmni Gwasg Rydd Caerdydd:** Publishers of political pamphlets in early seventies.

reasons for requesting this as did they, except that the organisation to which I belong is not at present killing and destroying;
one wonders cynically whether the fact that morally I am as
well qualified, will weigh as much as the fact that militarily I am
not as murderous, with the authorities. Knowing them —I doubt
it. I welcome your advice which is why I have given you the
full facts.

Safeguard your health, regards to all,

Er mwyn Cymru,

John

To Cyril Hodges

Annwyl Cyril,

I hope you are well and happy and that in this you are joined by your family.

Thank you for your letters, and again I beg your forgiveness for my tardy reply —due to the lack of letters available I fear.

I thought your poem magnificent, and I think your efforts on my behalf even more so. I thank you from the bottom of my heart for both, but I must add that my gratitude is tempered by concern at the way you ignore your physical limitations. I want you to be in a position to look out at Caerdydd when it is a dynamic centre of national aspirations and an exciting site of legislative and executive Welsh institutions; this will not be too ambitious, *if* you are prepared to admit the superiority of discretion, and the fact that even a will like yours must ultimately bow to human frailty. You have been an inspiration to me, and much too kind; and your philosophy has succeeded in, if not stopping me in my tracks, in making me re-evaluate my criteria and methods. This is no small thing, because you have succeeded where the entire Empire and State machine has failed. The fact that I am no longer a proscribed person in Wales is due in no small degree to your unique qualities as mediator. The people —our people, have my devotion and my dedication, and if the Cause requires it, they may have my life.

One point, I must clarify however —I am not a man of violence; I do not believe that anything was ever solved by the use of mindless violence. I abhor it, but I must admit to its efficacy when used against those who live by it and worship it. I deplore that I have ever had to resort to violence —but I deplore even more the conditions (created by an uncaring State in unknowing collision with an apathetic population) which necessitated such violence. One of the mind-boggling attributes

---

[1]H.M.Prison, Cambridge Road, Bristol: John Jenkins was transferred to H.M.P. Bristol for one month to receive accumulated visits.

of the Imperialist State is that its chief criterion of the emergence of political maturation, is the efficient application of the capacity and will to kill and destroy on the part of the subject people. That such a criterion can exist in this day and age is appalling; that its existence and proof can be ignored is worse.

I believe that violence or force, unorganised and unconnected with a political objective, is as abortive as a political movement seeking power without the means necessary to seize and retain it —if necessary. I must concede, in the final analysis, that the State's recognition of the fact that organised and efficient resistance to rule, if freedom isn't granted *must* be regarded as a political factor of the first magnitude. Moral and ethical considerations are of no avail when political power is at stake, as far as the State is concerned, although these qualities are prime motivators as far as the subject race is concerned. Therefore, I do not like violence; I deplore if —but I *must* recognise its efficacy, because the rules, made by the State which grants freedom, decree this, and therefore, ultimately I must be prepared to accept a short term moral volte-face in order to ensure the political and cultural survival and promotion of our people. But this is now an academic exercise, and is not for me; thanks to you I now have other interests, and although my objective has never altered, I am prepared to haggle on the strategy and tactics.

If I may, Cyril —business, or I will never get off the soapbox. The abstracts were coloured by me because I "felt" that the colours were "right". The first three were more an experimental splashing of colours, but the last ones were entirely deliberate, because I felt (like any other amateur) that I had mastered colours enough to temper blatant comparison with subtlety. I had reached the stage where I saw the "whole" picture and was able to put two colours, not really compatible, together, in the knowledge that their neighbours would temper the overall effect & create a "spicy" rather than a "sour" mix. I was not really restricted, but I *was* rather disappointed by the "quality" of the colours; I had hoped for the colours to be smooth, deep and well-toned e.g. the red to be like fresh blood and the green to be like lustrous grass, but when dry they appeared matt and a different shade. I accepted this and exploited it as far as possible.

Regarding Ned,[2] Cyril, as my mentor, I am delighted to offer you carte blanche in every way. You may use anything and everything and I object to nothing.

There is one favour I would ask of you (unless it has already been attended to by others). I was rather upset to hear that in 'Y Faner'[3] there were two *separate* appeals to friends to remember Ffred and friends,[4] and myself over the Christmas by sending us cards. There are two many schions in our ranks; as you say we must work in greater unison, so therefore I would be grateful if you could arrange *one* deliberately large insert in the 'Nation' giving the details of *all* of us behind bars for the Cause (bearing in mind that I shall be back at Albany by then). The success of the abstracts I am sure is due entirely to your ministrations, and as I said, you have carte blanche as to their disposal. Please give my thanks to M. Flincker for his expert advice. In the meantime, my regards to you all, and please — caution.

Er mwyn Cymru,
John

---

[2]Ned: Ned Thomas, Editor *Planet*. Cyril Hodges had asked John Jenkins for permission to send several letters along with commentary for publication in *Planet*. (See *Planet* 20)

[3]Y Faner: Welsh-language weekly newspaper.

[4]Ffred and friends: Ffred Ffransis and other Cymdeithas yr Iaith Gymraeg members in jail at the time.

1973

To Ned Thomas and Sara Erskine

Annwyl Ned a Sara,

I hope you are well and happy and that you enjoyed Christmas and the New Year performances.

Thank you very much for your respective letters and also for the 'Planet' editions. I enjoyed the Communes magazine and would welcome any more you have lying around. I was most grateful for the Celtic Art booklet which I have found absolutely invaluable; I have sent on three abstracts which I completed after digesting the booklet —no doubt you are able to assess the difference in technique already because although I haven't seen the earlier ones for some time they were executed in a measure which should have resulted in my joining them.

I am most gratified at the interest you both show in the projected *Moshav* and I hope that you were not being kind when you offered to help. In the building of Cymru, we all have our parts to play and the most efficient means of co-ordinating the process is to try to allocate to each his own particular craft in such a manner as to fit such work into the general pattern.

I will be blunt and confirm what you must know already. In order that this *Moshav* get off the ground, three factors are necessary —

1) Drive and enthusiasm & technical espertise.
2) Popular support.
3) Financial backing.

I am able to guarantee the first factor, but the responsibility for the remainder rests with those who are able to counterbalance the effects of the Mule and its drivelling minions. Another

factor to be taken into account is the emergence of the Welsh
Political Prisoners' Defence Committee in all its horror, because
in view of the rather overstated views of certain vocal leaders of
that otherwise excellent movement, the general effect regarding
myself is counter-productive. By being over vocal regarding my
methods, these people are committing the cardinal error of
moving forward too quickly and thereby alienating the general
public *whose support is necessary* for the completion of the
groundwork. Their actions are forcing people into a confrontation situation, because in the manner being used, approval for
me is consonant with disapproval of other factions. This is
polarising opinions at the wrong time and I now find that
instead of being benevolently accepted by the many, I am
being hysterically lauded as a cult figure by the few, and whereas this would be ideal, were I to be making a military stand outside this place, it is counter-productive in my efforts to attack
on the economic, cultural and political fronts.

To succeed, *I must* be in a position to ask *and receive* help —
physical help —from a large section of our non-slave-minded
young. To do this, I must be acceptable and credible, because
as the day of my release draws nearer I must assume that the
opposition, knowing well what success on the West Coast *really*
means, will use every means to discredit me. Even more
important is the idea itself —the idea of physically building our
land ourselves. I used to believe with Fanon that the fight to
achieve freedom from imperialist colonialism was what really
made men feel free rather than the trappings which accompany
the result. I still believe this —I must because I have personal
knowledge of it —but I feel now that the term "fight" need not
necessarily apply to simple physical action of an agressive or
defensive nature. It can equally well apply to the struggle to
achieve an economic, cultural or purely political objective,
providing that the work is hard and a measure of sacrifice is
acceptable and even desired for the Cause. I do not believe in
the "right" way or the "wrong" way in achieving our objective
of a Free, Welsh-speaking, Socialist Cymru; I strongly believe in
the winning way whichever way that is, always bearing in mind
that the methods of attack *must* be based on a rational and

60

logical assessment of the attitude and capability of those from whom we must take power. The fact that they have the power and a regard for the way they obtained it (and are keeping it in Ulster) must make it fairly obvious that the rules are not those of the Spasskys and Fischers but of the Hergisks and Horsas. I have said all this before, but I think that my point and plea must be clear to you both and I would be pleased to accept your very kind offers of help in that capacity at which you excel. The object is not to create a myth but to counter legend and thus give the project a chance —*which is all it needs.*

You are being more than kind by doing what you are at the moment. There is much to be said for the idea of respectability and more to be said for changing the criteria applicable to it; only when to love means to give and when respectability is the condition of having given and done, rather than crying one's eyes out in London, can we regard the basic foundation as having been laid. You have been given the blood and the chains:- describe the blood as the libation it truly was and make the chains gleam brighter than even thirty pieces of silver. Forgive please, my blatant disregard for Celtic curliques —this is a time for bluntness. Fraternal love.

> Er mwyn Cymru, (Sosialaidd a Chymraeg),
> John

P.S. Thanks for lovely card.

> J.

To Raymond Edwards

Annwyl Raymond,

It seems to me from the strange.letters[1] I have been reading recently that people like W.S.Parry and his friends live in a completely different world from the rest of us. Their world is one in which there is no suppression, all is subject to the laws of chivalry, ethics and morals and the meek will inherit the earth. In fact, political power is a drug which once taken creates a dependence worse than any hallucinogenic. There is no connection between political power and ethics, morals or legality and those who state otherwise are knaves while those who believe them are fools. The much-vaunted pen which is mightier than the sword is the one which signs the cheques and the death warrants.

Those who believe in the ethical motivation of our masters apparently believe that the granting of Independence is a simple matter automatically following th election of 19 or more Nationalist M.P.'s. I am called an Idealist and this is deserved, but I deal only in facts which are provable and *trends* which can be deduced, and the facts are as follows:-

1) Plaid Cymru has been functioning for nearly 50 years and has achieved very little.

2) It has been estimated that at the present rate of progress it will take a further 50 years to gain even half the Welsh seats.

3) Wales cannot wait that long, and therefore —

4) The strategy must be changed.

Contrary to W.S.Parry's belief, I am *not* a mad anarchist; I am a convinced constitutionalist which means that I hold and exercise the views expressed and exercised by every Nation State in the world today. All these States function according to two quite distinct and separate sets of laws; the one is the normal day to day code, *but* in the event that the survival of the

---

[1]**letters:** See letters from W.S.Parry, R.C.Kennard etc. in *Welsh Nation*, Plaid Cymru English-Language monthly magazine, February-July, 1973.

Nation, either by natural functions or by *attack* from outside, is threatened, then they all legally reserve the right to suspend the constitution, Democracy, Christianity or indeed anything else which could possibly inhibit the fight for survival. It is this law which is being wrongly quoted by England to Strasbourg to justify her gross and obscenely fascist fight to maintain her second Colony, and it is this law which justifies what I was forced to do for the survival of our little Nation. Pacifism, on the other hand, does not recognise the right to fight under *any* circumstances and insists on the dictum that it is better to be pas arrivé than nouveau riche; this is the idea which culminates in the Bishop going down in the sinking liner because he is too busy looking for his gaiters to board the lifeboat, and this is the same idea which bids us die like Gentlemen rather than live as men. I happen to believe that a new, free Welsh-Speaking Wales is worth fighting and even dying for, unlike those who are prepared to wait for a miracle; that we as Welsh people still remain a recognisably linguistic, social and ethnic entity is itself a miracle and we cannot hope for more unless we are prepared to make history rather than read it. When one goes to clean out the Augean Stables, one must expect to emerge eventually smelling rather less sweet than roses and spattered with rather more than sweat.

I am prepared to compromise myself for the sake of my country, and while I accept that there are those who are not prepared to risk their personal salvation for the National good, they in turn, must accept that the times call for more than they are willing to offer, and should therefore not seek to justify their hearthside heroics. I suppose it can be taken as progress of sorts that they seek to rationalise their stance by attacking the facts which prove otherwise.

In common with most other patriots, I claim the inalienable and constitutional right to bear arms in defence of my people and to fight for the survival of our identity and culture; the fact that I do so at the behest of my conscience and not as a result of some senior government official signing a piece of paper detracts neither from its legality or moral justification. People should not believe official propaganda, in which those like myself are classed as malcontents and troublemakers. The necessity for my commission of certain drastic acts came about as a direct result of others' omission of normal defensive acts over many years. I regretted my actions, but I regretted even more the conditions which made them necessary. I did not create the environment which created me; the environment evolved as a result of hundreds of years of pacifists relying on the goodwill of our masters, when a moment's thought should have been sufficient to demonstrate that had they been the fount of moral and ethical values, they could never have become our masters.

I must be regarded, as must Dafydd Iwan[2], Ffred Ffransis and my other fellow-members of Cymdeithas yr Iaith, as symptoms of an overall pattern rather than as causes of unrest. We who agitate must be seen in true historical perspective as part of a classic sequence which is as inevitable as the seasons; the reason for the spontaneous interest and action is due to the recognition of the vital importance of time and the National loss if the wait be too long.

I do not accept W.S.Parry's rebuke about my assumption that incarceration entitles me to moralise. I must point out that my letter was written in reply to a public statement by him in which he said that the M.A.C. campaign failed in its bid for public support. W.S.Parry feels entitled to write of events entirely foreign to him and of which he is completely ignorant, and then expresses hurt surprise when the person concerned tries *yet again* to straighten the record, and indeed accuses the innocent party of abusing his position in prison to moralise. Yet again in his latest letter, he questions the efficacy of the M.A.C. campaign of direct action; I do not wish to be hurtful but when W.S.Parry clearly does not know the objective of the exercise, he is hardly in a position to query the tactics, strategy or results of the campaign. My love for my country is not conditional and neither would my actions be motivated by anything other than a desire to execute my duties as a loving, loyal and totally dedicated Cymro. I do not regard the terms

---

[2]**Dafydd Iwan:** Chairman, Cymdeithas yr Iaith Gymraeg (1968-71) and folk singer.

'Fanatic' and 'Ruthless' as denigration, but as necessary qualities which must be utilised to harness the goodwill of the people to the application necessary to formulate and execute any action necessary to attain the National objective.

The fact that I am in prison I regard as merely a necessary phase which cannot be regarded in isolation as a failure, but which must be seen and assessed in the terms of the overall picture. It can be regarded as a failure in the way that a momentary glimpse of Hastings in 1066 during which the Normans were executing their 'retreat' could be described as an English Victory. The killing of the leaders of the Easter Rebellion of 1916 did not signify defeat for the Cause as such, any more than the death of Christ on the Cross betokened the end for Christianity.

Prison for revolutionaries is a time-honoured and accepted phase because this is where the sheep are separated from the goats, and where those who do and those who say, finally part. Saunders Lewis has written that the road to Freedom runs through the prison gates, and this is true because the cell is in the front line of Welsh Political Action. It is also a fact that the Nationalist in prison adds a new dimension to Patriotism and a new qualification for Cymreictod. The Nationalist free to the Nationalist in prison is the Army Cadet to the hardened veteran. It is easy to be a Christ on Palm Sunday but there is more merit in those who will face a Good Friday; therefore although my prison ordeal may not entitle me to dispense moral judgements upon those whose philosophy is not entirely compatible with my own, if I do so decide, they have a greater validity than those from without. The discussion does not hinge on philosophic points but on facts, figures, love and action:

a) Wales is dying —Fact.
b) 500 years of Pacifism has been counter-productive —Fact.
c) 6 years of agitation have been more productive than the previous 600 —Fact.

W.S.Parry also misinterprets my remarks about the Cause moving forward on more than one front. Any Cause, in order to succeed must move forward on the Political, Economic, Cultural and Military fronts; that is, the Cause must have a practical vision of a new society, the financial means and brains to sustain the struggle, the bitterness of cultural deprivation and the love of cultural heritage, and finally the means and will to use the ultimate sanction if necessary to achieve the objective. I do not see that the Caradog Pritchards, the Emlyn Williams', the Goronwy Rees', the Richard Burtons, the Tom Jones' and Shirley Basseys et al[3], in all the glory of their Berkshire and Surrey homes, do much for Welsh Speaking Free and Socialist Wales.

As for R.C. Kennard, I simply cannot understand the points he is trying to make. I am a simple peasant, but I suspect that neither he nor W.S.Parry will ever be present at a confrontation, the main qualification for which will be the ability to achieve a political objective by military means, which includes the will and means to shed blood, and if History is the judge, this will have been proved *before* the confrontation.

Let us therefore agree amicably to differ; he is the expert on facing a vote of censure from the Council and I am more used to facing death. If W.S.Parry undertakes to stop fulminating from the fireside, attacking from the armchair and sermonising from the sofa, then I will try to stop pontificating (unless provoked) from the prison. Hwyl.

Er mwyn Cymru,
John

---

[3] Caradog Pritchard; Emlyn Williams and Richard Burton; Goronwy Rees; Tom Jones and Shirley Bassey: Welsh journalist and novelist; actors; writer and former Principal U.C.W. Aberystwyth; singers respectively.

To Cyril Hodges

Annwyl Cyril,

I hope that you and yours are well and happy.

Thank you for your latest letter which I was very pleased (and relieved) to receive. It was extremely reassuring to discover that you and Ifan were able to survive and flourish on the frank and useful and prolonged chat you both underwent all over that weekend. I was delighted to hear that all went well, through the earlier card, and that the project was over its first hurdle.

I believe that sea farming, or 'aquaculture' as it is apparently called, is the industry of the future, and not only on the economic plane, because it is part of a constant and continuous cycle. It makes economic *and* ecological sense, and proves that the necessary viability need not rely on exploitation of a blind and once-only nature. It will prove that the 'Fast Buck' principle is counter-productive and indeed self-destructive in the long term, and these days above all others we must plan on a long-term basis.

I sincerely hope that you are right in your belief that the idea will be copied over and over again, because with you I believe that the economic and therefore the cultural future of our land must be gradually undertaken by us, if there is to be any hope of survival. This is why it is so desperately necessary that this project succeed, because nothing succeeds like success and this effort must be the prototype of the rest.

But however desperate one becomes for manpower, one should not recruit the hippies and yippies; in my opinion there is no more efficient method of damning the whole operation, and putting the cause back at least ten years which cannot be spared. I never really knew much about these types before I was captured, but having been forced to mix with them I am now an unwilling authority on the subject. Wales requires those who are able to assess and progress, whereas the dictum of the hippy is to assess —then digress; they seem to be unable to face realism, rather preferring to remain in a constant state of drugs-induced euphoria. They talk of themselves as Revolutionaries but their only quarrel with the State is that their habit is illegal; all their talk of marching on the authorities if it ever actually came about could be stopped in its tracks by dropping a ton or two of marijuana and declaring it legal. They are not potential revolutionaries but frustrated fascists.

I hope I have not given the impression lately, Cyril, that I am biased against those who are relatively pacifist; if, for no other reason, I could not afford this attitude because this section of the Cymry has been very good to me and has demonstrated its understanding and affection in many ways. Now and again, I must look out at the odd venomous pygmy who demonstrates his courage by spitting on the grave of men who were in every way his superior except in sense —but again who ever succeeded in anything using logic as an essential criterion?

I have great sympathy with the genuine pacifist who would sacrifice all for his beliefs, but I occasionally get the impression that there are those who use the beliefs as justification for their armchair stance. I do not particularly object to passengers but I do not like being stabbed in the back by those in the rear seat. There comes a time when one must choose between two evils, and then one chooses the lesser and always the method which will show the best results in the long term for the greatest number. No-one *wants* to see another Ulster, but if the alternative is deracination and cultural genocide then I will always take the way which will leave my children no reason to regard me in the bitter way I regard my expedient ancestors. A friend of mine for whom I have a high regard and a deep respect for his pacifist views, said the other day "But your way would result in a Wales where for years, the vendetta and recriminations would be the norm". This is probably true and regrettable, but I would think it to be infinitely preferable to the alternative which I regard as the inevitable consequence of inaction. I believe we all have a part to play and the greatest part is toleration which means the ability to admit that perhaps one is wrong and then to move over. I do not object to fighting other people's battles for them and I do not object to going to prison for their lack of action. But when 'they' then attack me using the very phrases of our masters, it is clear that the propaganda of the other side is very strong or that 'they' are very weak.

We must get the pigs out of the vineyard and I cannot see that being achieved by reasoned tolerant discussion, which has been tried time and time again. How anyone can advocate this course of action alone after Tryweryn I simply cannot understand.

I hope your renaissance of better health continues Cyril, to enable you to continue in your well-suited role of eminence grise. My sincere regards to you and yours. Hwyl.

                    Er mwyn Cymru,
                    John

P.S. A friend informs me that designs and colours take more readily and clearly on book covers of linen cloth than on normal gloss paper? ?

                    J.

To Robat Gruffudd

Annwyl Robat,

I hope you and Elwyn are well and happy.

Thank you very much for "Nabod Cymru" which I received today; it is very kind of you to remember me. I hope you received the three designs I sent off a couple of weeks ago —the "carchar" card and two cardiau Nadolig, and that they are of some use. I have today sent off another, (this time by registered post, so it may take a little longer to reach you) and this one includes a Celtic cross and two ranges of colours. If, however, you wish to change any colours, please do so. This latest card is rather ambiguous and could be used either as a carchar card or a cerdyn Nadolig, (or perhaps both); if you feel it could be of use, do as you wish with it. Just a thought —if you perhaps feel that the sentence ending "dros Gymru" is a little too long-winded, do you think that the single phrase "Keep the Faith" (yn Gymraeg) would suffice?

I expect you are in touch with Gwynfor's[1] family, including his latest son-in-law[2]; would you be kind enough to give him my fraternal greetings and comradely regards. One only hopes that as so much is being done to save the language by a few, that they will in turn receive the complementary assistance of those who should be taking action to save the people who speak it. But, unfortunately our land is full of those who believe that the Augean stables can be cleaned out thoroughly while leaving the cleaners unspattered and indeed smelling like roses. They do not understand that security for the vine grower means fences for the pigs, and that peaceful persuasion will not clear out greedy swines. So in Cymru we struggle on, economically making guns for "them" before butter for us, and politically casting pearls before swine when perhaps a boot up the backside

---

[1]Gwynfor: President of Plaid Cymru. M.P. for Carmarthen (1966-70), (1974-79). First Plaid Cymru M.P. to be elected.

[2]**his latest son-in-law:** Ffred Ffransis, husband of Gwynfor Evans' daughter Meinir.

would be more fitting and certainly more efficacious. I will stop now before launching into a sermon. Hwyl.

> Er mwyn Cymru,
> John

To Sara Erskine

Annwyl Sara,

I hope you and your family are well and happy.

Many thanks for your letter and Planet 17 both of which I found stimulating and helpful as usual. I was unable to acknowledge receipt via Cyril as I have not heard from him for months —I believe him to be ill again and would be grateful for news. He is a critical link to me both personally and by way of the project and I am extremely worried by his silence.

The last letter I received from him was after the 'technical experts' had visited him to explain the basic outline of the project, and it met with Cyril's full approval for its potential — both economically and ideologically. He could see that it maintained a full ecological circle whereby one did not exploit and exit, but reared, reaped, replaced and maintained in a manner beneficial to the pocket and nature.

I am not quite sure how to react to the incredible rash of movements, organisations and their accompanying organs these days. The sudden emergence of United Welsh Action, Mudiad Gwerin Cymru, Welsh Socialist Vanguard, W.P.P.D.C. et al., with the Hosts of Rebecca, Free Wales, Y Gweriniaethwr and so on, certainly reflect a resurgence of either the National Welsh Spirit, or a realisation of the crisis which hovers, and our unpreparedness to face it or the realities of life. Either way is shown an indictment either of Plaid Cymru or of its party machine regarding the dissemination of Party Policy, and I find this very regrettable and also very dangerous, because above all else, the centuries of domination have taught us that sincerity, sacrifice, belief in the Cause, and love for the people is not enough. Discipline, organisation and application will always win, and although might is not right, organised might will always be superior to disorganised right. Unity is strength and strength is survival as a people; disunity and personality cults will ensure the survival of individuals who will have much to regret, a heritage to bury and many wreaths to lay. Disunity is not so much a bouquet laid on the shrine of rugged individuality, as a wreath laid on the tomb of Welsh aspirations. Ours is not a land of slaves; it is worse, it is a land peopled by 2½ million presidents.

Luckily, at present, these new groups are not political competition because they regard themselves as pressure groups who will not contest elections on any level; but the fact of their existence points to a rising awareness that Plaid Cymru is no longer in the van, and this augurs ill for the future.

I regard the recent elections[1] as illustrating the essential weakness of the Blaid —that is of trying to fight and win elections on goodwill to personalities rather than on good Socialist policies. Unfortunately the Blaid cannot fight on good Socialist policies because the party contains so many eminent academics and culture vultures who are basically non-Socialist. The attitude is —"We are all of differing creeds, but we have united in the desire for Freedom. On attaining Freedom we will then split up into our respective factions." *But* Freedom will *never* be attained by a movement which is not radically Socialist, because in Wales this is the *only* party which will get the votes of the werin. In the recent elections, results proved that the Blaid did well in the areas where culture was of prime importance, and also in areas where personalities fought as individuals who were known and admired for their stand for the people. The elections were proof that overall, the public did not regard the Blaid as a good, viable and radical alternative to the Labour Party, because the basic Socialist Welsh creed was not sufficiently emphasized. There *must* be a happy medium between rugged individuality and Father-Figure-with-children; there must also be a happy medium between culture vulture and the wild hairy with his little red book. There must be a norm somewhere between the fey and the fanatic where they neither receive the Freedom of the City not wear leg-irons. And the tragedy is that unless the Blaid are able to produce this basic policy before people run out of patience, Wales will again become a victim to the quality which has ensured her survival.

---

[1] **recent elections:** County Council Elections, April 1973; District Council Elections, May 1973.

We have been praying for rain and we may yet drown in the flood.

I am still regularly receiving the "Llais"[2] for which continuing thanks (but I wish to God that Ned were the Editor).

As usual, I apologise for the tardiness of this reply which as usual says so little about so much. My most sincere regards. Keep the Faith. Hwyl.

Er mwyn Cymru,
John

---

[2]**Llais y Sais:** ('Voice of the English') i.e. *Western Mail.*

To Cyril Hodges

Annwyl Cyril,

I hope that you and your family are well and happy.

Many thanks for your latest letter which I was very pleased to receive, illustrating as it does your firm grip on your personal affairs and your continuing benevolent safeguarding of the interests of Cymru.

I must agree with your description of George Thomas, Elystan Morgan et al. as noxious reptiles. They are the worms of Wales and they nourish themselves on the dead hopes of our gentle people; their houses are built on foundations made of the gravestones of our aspirations, and their ladders to success are made from our bones. However, there is more to life than logic and logistics; progress and the better things of life occur in spite of, not because of, the trends and patterns forecast by the experts who are consistently wrong in their attempt to reduce the human condition to a mathematical equation and to reproduce the soul on a drawing board.

I remember attending a meeting at which Elystan Morgan[1] announced his defection from the Blaid in order to change everything from within the party of power. Unfortunately, he spoke yn Gymraeg, and by the time I found out what he had said, the moment to interrupt had gone. He went on about the illogicality of trying to achieve success without power, and he used logical argument to justify his position; unfortunately for his logic, several months later Gwynfor made history at Caerfyrddin, which was not really very sporting or logical of him, or the people who put him there.

I therefore have as much respect for logic of that sort as I have for the dogma of certain communists, or in fact for any of the Communist regimes. As you say, the Chinese version *is* the lesser of two evils, but any movement which has lost its

---

[1]Elystan Morgan: Labour M.P. for Ceredigion (1966-74). Had previously been a prominent member of and prospective parlimentary candidate for Plaid Cymru.

integrity, faith and altruistic motivation, and replace these qualities with powerful party machinery and sterile deadly dogma, is a power for evil in the world. I would place in this category not only the Communist regimes, but the totalitarian ones, the organised religious institutions and the so-called "major" political parties of England. I believe that there is possible a system where men may achieve happiness and a good life in conditions which will in fact approximate to those hoped for, prayed for, but not worked for, by Christians. This Utopian condition can only be achieved by a Nation/State of a certain size, peopled by a race with a capacity for faith and self-sacrifice; the smallest nations cannot achieve the financial viability and the largest are too riven with class and sectional interests. Therefore, those qualities which the experts have declared to be weaknesses, are in fact the strong foundations upon which the Welsh Socialist Utopia may be built, namely the enormous reservoir of irrational faith, and the minuteness of Wales as a spatial concept.

Please forgive the sermon, Cyril, it is just that I have received a body blow with the latest figures[2] for the Welsh-speakers, and I am inclined to lash out at those who apparently believe that culture is an isolated subject, and that a cultural problem has a cultural cause which naturally has a cultural cure. In fact, Wales suffers from cultural deprivation caused by economic neglect caused by political mismanagement, (and in that last factor I believe I am being very, very generous), and to attempt to cure the cultural problem by initiating a language council, is analogous to putting a poultice on a boil caused by a blood defect. To remove a symptom is not to allay the cause, and one is entitled to query the sincerity of those who lend themselves to this farce. I too, pay respect to the old dark gods of mist, earth and air; the concept of a sacred soil has been devalued by recent demagogues, but their use of the term concerned power, prestige and profit rather than veneration and should be considered accordingly.

My friend (whose name I must not mention by regulations)

---

[2] latest figures: Results of Census of 1971 published on the 1st of October October, 1973.

was very pleased that Pegi liked his work. He has asked me to express his gratification at her approval and to ask you with all deference if you would allow him to make her a gift of it with his sincere respects.

You are, as usual, over-modest when you say that you have been most fortunate in having recent work accepted. I do not understand how a poet works, for the simple reason that I am not God; I believe that poetry cannot be explained in logical mundane terms, but that it is the proof of minds on a different, more beautiful and infinitely satisfying level. I believe that poetry and good music is divinely inspired and a visible sign of divine inspirations; how fortunate to be beloved and favoured of the Gods. I often read the books of your poetry which you were kind enough to send me Cyril, and I greatly enjoy them every time. Best wishes —Hwyl a hedd to you all.

Er mwyn Cymru,
John

To Cyril Hodges

H.M.Prison
Albany
10 December 1973

Annwyl Cyril,

I hope that you and yours are well and happy.

I write this tardy and compact couple of lines after just reading the account of our correspondence in the latest "Planet". As a friend remarked to me: "That article bears the unmistakable stamp of a master-craftsman who deals in words". I am very pleased indeed with the article; it sets everything in the correct perspective and with a minimum of words covers volumes. Thank you sincerely for being so very kind and I admire greatly your perspicacity and intellect (added to a deft touch of political application) in effectively removing me from one sphere of operations to another, where in order to achieve more I have to do less.

You have achieved single-handed what the authority and agencies of the State could not; you have removed my venom, and have placed a quite comfortable velvet glove on a nailed fist. "They" will not be pleased because they would have preferred to render me impotent by *dis*crediting me; you have taken me out of the front line and rendered me as a creator rather than a destroyer —by *acc*rediting me.

I have learned that a revolutionary fire is essential, *but* to be utilised efficiently as a creative force, must be contained within the fireplace of discipline and surrounded by the fireguard of organisation. Without these, it is a great force for destruction, but these without the fire, represents decadence and stagnation and a fight for power solely as a means to attain more power.

I enclose my personal Christmas card. It bears the religious motif for several reasons (to do with Celtic Art being tied up with the Church, and to draw attention to Welsh association with an earlier 'permanent' Empire, but mainly to take the tinsel out of an event and to try to restore it to some simplicity. on principle). I will close now Cyril, offering you again my sincere and grateful thanks for your great help in 1973. Hwyl a hedd.

Er mwyn Cymru,
John

To Sara Erskine

Annwyl Sara,

I hope that you are, with Ned and the children, well and happy, and that you enjoyed Christmas in spite of the festivities.

Thank you for your letter which, as usual, I found very interesting and tending to spark off a delightful discussion of too great a dimension to cover in a few pages. Anyway, to answer your queries:-

a) The Western Mail. I was delighted to hear that we have tentacles even there; by all means let sleeping dogs lie, and who better at lying than the W. Mail.

b) "Celtic Art" by George Bain. I recently received a copy* from Lolfa who appear to like my humble efforts. (Thank you also for your very kind comments on my latest card). The unfortunate thing about Celtic Art as an Art, is that it is inseparable from Christianity and cannot be secularised very successfully. However, as Celtic art draws attention to our roots and separate development, I must regard it as a political factor and endeavour to assist in bringing about a Celtic Art revival to run parallel with the resurgence of Lit. and Lang. in my own humble fashion. (This all sounds terribly pompous except that I mean it and I have to be so concise in the space allowed.)

c) The card for the two ladies. They have since sent me a card so I have been able to send them another. If you have it still, might I suggest that it be sent to a friend on the W. Mail.

d) The £5. As I cannot spend it on your children (unless you have changed your mind since —the offer is still open) perhaps you could forward it to me here. I sent off my last £1 to the fund for the "Shrewsbury 24"[1] and I could do with some more, if you would be so kind.

e) The Language and Politics question. I apologise for giving the over-simplistic answer that the Welsh language will cease to be a problem when there is no political suppression; in fact the problem will be immense because of the almost fatal imbalance which will probably be much worse by then. But the machinery of the State will then be actively encouraging not passively ignoring as at present. I agree with you that socialism with a small "s" is not political but a philosophy of life, but I believe that Socialism with a large "S" creates the conditions in which one may practise this philosophy. All "isms" are systems of priority in the same way that all politics deal with power; I believe that Socialism —true Socialism which has never yet been allowed on this planet —is the only system which would encourage culture at the expense of profits and which would see happiness as the criterion of good government rather than the materialistic imperialism which is eating us alive. It is not the output of millionaires but the shortfall of beggars which decides on the form and worth of society.

If the problem were mine, which thank God it is not, then I would set my sights on 1 million monoglot Welsh-speakers within three generations. I could give a blueprint, but it would take too much space, but it basically depends on extending the base of the Cymraeg monoglot, with the emphasis on prestige rather than status. I agree with the present struggle of C y I G for status because the enemy is the State, but when the State is friendly then prestige is the goal. Status is to do with the position in the framework of the State; prestige is to do with the feelings of the people. During his great days, George Thomas, as the most powerful and highest ranking Government official in Wales had unequalled status; —but prestige?

To regard culture as *only* cultural and needing no political roots is to regard an ideology which is allowed to exist inside the framework of power, as successful. Cultural Nationalism in Wales on these terms would thus be reduced to the state of effectiveness of the C of E in England; an organisation which has power by association, status by law, an elite priesthood by

[1]The Shrewsbury 24: A reference to the case of the Trade Unionists arrested in October and November 1972 during the construction workers' strike at Shrewsbury of whom six were charged with conspiracy, unlawful assembly and affray. For further details see: *The Shrewsbury Three: Strikes, Pickets and 'Conspiracy'* by Jim Arinson. London: Lawrence and Wishart, 1974.

custom, and which is almost totally irrelevant to the daily pagan life of the people, *and which has therefore failed*.

There *is* an inspiring and effective policy for Cymraeg without kiss-of-death compulsion but that is another story. If the future leaders in Wales can be Socialist and uncorrupted by power that *would* be a miracle; in case there *is* no miracle then what is wrong with a "Mao-type" cultural, and therefore blood-less, revolution every time mellowness sets in to betray the cause? More later. Sincere regards. Hwyl a Hedd.

> Er mwyn Cymru,
> John

*But many thanks for your very kind offer. I am touched.

1974

H.M.Prison
Albany
17 January 1974

To Sara Erskine

Annwyl Sara,

I hope that you are well and happy, and that Ned and the children are also.

Many thanks for your letter which desolated me with the sad news[1] about Cyril. Due to the weather, your letter which was posted on 5th Jan, did not reach here until the 10th, but immediately on receipt I wrote a letter of sympathy to poor Pegi.

I am still shattered, so perhaps you will understand the brevity of this letter and forgive. I am most grateful for your interest and help regarding the designs. I really have no idea of their commercial possibilities or their aesthetic worth and I would be delighted to give you carte blanche for them, if you feel inclined to accept yet another burden on my behalf. As I remember it, the earlier ones were pretty awful and hardly worth showing, but I will leave that in your and Dafydd Gwyn's hands. The last one I drew, the Chi-Rho, has been framed and given to my younger son Rhodri, but if you wish to show it, I will ask him to send it to you.

The one thing I fear is that people will say nice things about them because they don't wish to offend me, but will think other things. The attitude I take is that they can be shown as:- (a) an example of what *can* be done in prison in spite of everything, or (b) an example of artistic work to be compared with anything else, *if they are* good enough. Unfortunately, I do not have the knowledge, so I will leave that with confidence to you. You and Ned are really so embarrassingly kind and practically

[1] **sad news: Cyril Hodges died January 1974.**

82

helpful that I do not know what I would have done in the past four years without you both.

Frang MacThomais of the Comunn na Canain Albannaich[2] wrote me a most interesting letter on the upsurge of interest in (and therefore the increased use of) Celtic Art in the Highlands. I am trying to promote the subject at Rhydfelen[3] via Eileen Beasley who is interested and knows something about it. In some ways they are rather conservative there, but surely the production of an end product which involved Latin, Welsh, Geometry and Art should be encouraged. I will write of Cyril later when I am rational. Hwyl. (P.S. I received one credit for 1st Year Foundation Course in O.U. 6 credits = B.A.)

Er mwyn Cymru,
John

---

[2]Comunn na Canian Albannaich: Scots Language Society.

[3]Rhydfelen: Bilingual Comprehensive School, Rhydfelin, Mid-Glamorgan.

To Dedwydd Jones

Annwyl Dedwydd,

I hope you are fulfilled and inspired rather than well and happy. Many thanks for your last letter, and many apologies for the delay in answering, but I have been going through one of the depressive stages which are endemic here.

Many thanks for your beautiful "The Women of Pilleth" which should be an enormous success in Islam, but not, I feel in America. Clearly, the crucible from which you have brilliantly emerged was formed by unfeeling and deadly amazons, and no doubt they will have deserved the intoxicating flow of enchanting poison which beautify the bitter pages. I agree with every word, and I am grateful that you are not a contented and satiated product of a crach-orientated society. The work you are doing is invaluable and will stand you in very good stead in the future, particularly regarding your ambition to establish the first National Movement of Welsh Drama. However, the Welsh Mafia, (*our* side that is) being what it is, it is as important to belong to the right section as it is to be versatile and talented, and perhaps an introduction or two may help. Around Easter, a friend of mine from the North will be in your area, and will call for a chat if that is convenient for you. You will have a great deal in common. He is *not* one of those people who believe that cultural freedom is possible within the present politico-economic framework; he believes, as do I, that freedom in those circumstances is as efficacious as a licence to plant potatoes in the desert.

As for me, I was born in Cardiff and bred in the valleys, but I was as untypical a product of my socialisation process as were you; by all the rules applicable, neither nurture nor nature could be credited with the final product. But, the feeling of dedication, of a mysterious fate were always present, even at an early age. I was always aware of the beast slouching to his birthplace, and I was aware tangibly at the secret places of communion. Even during the hot and dark years of puberty, in between the strident and imperative surges of the mad and thrilling blood, I was aware of a faint and sweet memory and of a sadness and yearning which could not be solely attributed to hormonal imbalance.

There were places which I knew were sacred and others which were filled with horror, but over all the overpowering déjà-vu and sense of continiuty, which always made me weak with love and surge with strength.

When I was 14, I took the Roman Road called Heol Adda, to the top of Gelligaer mountain. This is the road which runs from the Auxiliary camp at Gelligaer to Brecon and beyond, but I did not know this at the time. I stood there at the top and looked round at the marvellous view which was enhanced by a blue sky and a bright sun. Suddenly and breathtakingly a cloud raced over the sun and an immense shadow filtted over all the land, and as I saw the shadow racing towards me across the bare mountain, I was filled with inexpressible grief and the certain knowledge that I had been there before at a time of great sadness and deprivation, and that I had seen the great shadow enveloping me then also. I think that the beast shook himself then and started to move according to his instinct; it could have been nothing else.

Unfortunately, in my experience, our people seem to be possessed of visionary and practical ability, but the visionaries are apt to catch their bollocks in the barbed wire, and the practical ones realise that the objective is impossible. I accept that it is not practicable to go to heaven on a rainbow, *but* the long path from the swamps and the caves is bordered by the bones of experts and littered by logical deductions founded on facts, which foundered on faith and will; it is also red with the blood always necessary to achieve socio-political change.

Strength is weakness and weakness is strength, when used properly. The strength of the (Fellahin)[1] lies in their unity in desiring the baubles to festoon themselves; their weakness is that they will accept the baubles from anyone who has them, or who seems to have the potential to have them. No principles,

---

[1] Fellahin: Egyptian peasants, here used as non-complimentary description of the cultured Anglo-Welsh.

no ethics, just big grasping hands feeling for coins and groins.
I enjoyed your "Bless the Giver". I hope you received the
Xmas card I sent and made. (Sorry about its non-secular
content but Celtic Art is barbaric and Christian —any stick to
beat the enemy, even one with a crossbar.) Regards dear
brother.

Er mwyn Cymru,
John

To Robat Gruffudd

Annwyl Robat,

I hope that you and Elwyn are well and happy.

Thank you for your recent thought-provoking letter which I will now answer before going on to the inevitable political discourse. I was pleased to hear that a profit was made on the cards, as much for the sake of Y Lolfa as for the beneficiaries.

I agree with you on the point of colours not being necessary; you will by now have received the two card designs in B & W. I must explain that they are, as you will have noted, both of the same Biblical passage —the difference being in the style of lettering. The one in straight letters appears to be unfinished, but as with the "Big A" Xmas card, one of the peculiarities of a Celtic page is that it consists of a large initial, sometimes (not always) a border, and usually only a word or two of the text. So that one is perfectly in order from the purist point of view; of course the technique and design are open to criticism and no-one realises that more than me. The curved letter one, it strikes me, could almost be used for a poster —if you feel there could be a demand for that sort of thing I would do another based on the size of the one you sent (for which many thanks). I welcome your comments. By the way, I deliberately used a green border on the one design, based on a calculation that the result your end would be a mid-grey, to make a little change from B & W. (If you decide to use it, that is.) Perhaps it would be another "Keep the Faith" card? for the Maes.

I was most interested to hear of your proposed poster on the apocalyptic theme; I would love to try something like that but unfortunately I am one of those people who cannot draw except in the abstract.

About bilingualism, I entirely agree. There can be no parity between tongues, particularly when one represents power & prestige and the other poetry & peasants*. I believe in Bilingualism as the lesser of two evils —it is better than linguistic

---

*That is to those properly socialised —English education.

genocide and a step in the right direction. If I were responsible for culture in an independent Cymru, my firm committment would be to produce a minimum of 1 million monoglot Welsh-speakers within three generations; anything less is only playing with the problem. The trick would be to compel without compulsion, but this is true of all political moves in fact.

About Dafydd Iwan's standing for Môn.[1] There have always been the two ideas about this; the one says that he should be elected, then he should refuse to attend the Parliament because of its irrelevance and his impotence. The other says he should go there and do his best in the circumstance.

We must always remember, when weighing up the pros and cons, the ultimate objective —Freedom. One can *not* achieve popular support unless the people acknowledge one's credibility, sincerity and reasonableness. When I say "popular support" I mean of course, for the Revolution, because that is the *only* way Freedom can be obtained. Whereas you and I and some others realise the impotence of even a good Welsh M.P., the moment when national consciousness is raised is when the *people* realise it. Our strategy must be to utilize *all* the channels of communication, *all* the means of redress, *all* the levers of power, until *all* democratic means have been *completely* exhausted: then even the most armchair bound, pipe-smoking, Morris 1000-driving, geranium-growing person will realise the total impotence of justice and the irrelevance of the corridors of power to our people. *Then*, the people will be behind one, and *then* one can win. Tryweryn & Clywedog proved *my* case for me. One must always be morally superior to the opposition, and never allow him to state that "Of course if those people had gone through the correct channels etc. etc." It is not enough for a group of aware people to antagonise the State; the strategy *must* be to educate the people so that a confrontation between them and the State becomes inevitable, and in the meantime to form and build an efficient spearhead to implement the people's eventual wishes. To educate the people one *must* move step by careful step, and one *must* be seen by

---

[1]**standing for Môn:** Dafydd Iwan contested Môn (Anglesey) for Plaid Cymru in the two elections of 1974.

the people to move step by careful step: then when they urge, one may break into a trot, some in front of the people, *and some behind.* Any hope that a confrontation between State and Nation was not inevitable, died the death on the day oil was found off our coast. The reason why people should vote for its freedom is an even more pressing reason for its denial by the State. One cannot blame the State for placing its survival and economic interests above all else; one must blame the Nation for not doing likewise.

Naturally, Robat, the above does not really concern the Gymdeithas which is a pressure group, interested in cultural matters and not in political power. It *does* concern political groups. Hwyl.

> Er mwyn Cymru,
> John

H.M.Prison
Albany
20 June 1974

To Raymond Edwards

Annwyl Raymond,

I hope that you, Kitt and the boys are in good health and are happy.

Many thanks for your latest letter and for the extract from "Y Faner" & the Obituary for Cyril. Thank you also for your kind remarks about my humble efforts at Christmas cards; people keep asking me to produce this type or that type of drawing, but I have found that the only type I feel able to undertake is connected with the early Christian era. I like to feel that I am helping to acquaint our people with their roots and heritage in a way which is not archaic but relevant to today, and quite frankly I am at a loss to comprehend why such a vast reservoir of beauty has been left untapped. Or could it be that there are those who do not wish people to be reminded of their culture because of its political undertones? —but perhaps I am being over-suspicious, and perhaps it is true that British History is to do with people watching spiders and burning cakes. Perhaps! What *is* certain is that British Democracy means that one has complete freedom to rattle one's chains and Law & Order ensures that no-one may stop one exercising this freedom.

It was good of Kitt to write to head office about Home Leave for me, and perhaps I should explain the system a little more fully. The person you refer to, who received Home Leave was here for some time, but was De-categorised as a Cat. 'B' prisoner, which is why he was able to go to Maidstone and receive this leave. The salient point is that while I am on the 'A' list I am *not* eligible for Hostel, Parole, Home Leave or any other sort of rehabilitation; I therefore expect to serve my full sentence of 10 years with remission which will be 6yrs 8mths, and have reconciled myself to this. Had I not been on the 'A' list I would have been eligible for parole over a year ago, but facts are facts, and the fact is that no 'A' man has ever received parole, and under existing regulations there is *no* possibility that he can do so.

Presumably, (and I am guessing because I have never been told why I am an 'A' man, or indeed what action is necessary to be removed from the list) I must accept one of two theories if I am to be recategorised.

1) That it is a good thing for Cymru to die, or
2) That there is an effective and democratic, and legal way of reversing the fatal process.

If I can accept either of these, then by the token of my acceptance, I also accept that my activities were uncalled for. All this is naturally hardly compatible either with my integrity or the historical facts, and therefore I have no alternative but to accept the present position. However, in the event that our Irish brothers and sisters are given recognition of their political status, which seems very likely at present, then I shall have to reconsider my position and my aspirations in that light. I would have to regard my unchanged status as a direct affront to Welsh Nationhood, and would have to act accordingly to secure parity of treatment.

I expect you were as shocked as was I, by the very sad end of Micky Gaughan,[1] a good friend to me and to our Cause. He was a very gentle and modest person, who, every year since he came to this prison, would demonstrate his solidarity by attending the special Communion Service for Dewi Sant at the Anglican Church, while I would reciprocate by attending the Special Mass for Padric Sant at the Catholic Church. Father Laverty, the priest, could never quite understand why Padric, if born in what is now the Lowlands of Scotland, must have been a Cymro.

I was very upset to hear about Cyril Hodges' very sad death; his passing was a sad event for the Cause, because he was one of the few who understood that right and wrong are relative concepts in the specific context of politics, and that sometimes it is a greater evil to sin by omission than by commission. sometimes feel that our ship of State has more to fear from the dogma of the dogmatics than from the fervour of the fanatics;

---

[1] **Micky Gaughan:** I.R.A. prisoner known to John Jenkins while at Albany who died as a result of his hunger strike on June 4th, 1974.

one hopes that the Captain will utilise any breeze in a calm, rather than go to any port in a storm.

Thank you for your very kind offer of help regarding reading materials. In fact, Cyril was not responsible for the "Nation"; that has always been very efficiently seen to by Dafydd Williams at P.C. I must admit that I really had no idea who was responsible for the W. Mule, until you mentioned it. I cannot ask you to get that because it is too expensive, but if you could secure for me an order for the "Wrexham Leader" I would be very grateful. I was getting it for the last 6 months but it has now run out.

I am not going to waste words on my reaction to "their" attitude to Kilbrandon, rates, road signs or anything else, because my reaction is as predictable as theirs. My reaction to their reactionary inaction is to enact action, not by traction but by impaction. And I agree with you and Jac Wiliams and Meredydd Edwards about the 4th channel. Anything that Geo. Thomas & Leo Abse approve *cannot* be good. Love to boys. Hwyl.

Er mwyn Cymru,
John

To Dedwydd Jones

Annwyl Dedwydd,

I hope that you and yours are happy and in good health.

Many thanks for your encouraging letter and for "Bard" which I found spellbinding. You stock your words like a well-filled bar, then mix them with the hand of a master to produce a brew as entrancing as it is intoxicating and as deadly as it is delicious. To me the result is nectar, but to those who lurk in the catacombs of Cardiff, feasting on their fat, it is a nauseous nitric acid, stripping off their pretentions and revealing their plastic bones connected by clichés and bound by Band-of-Hope platitudes. Their creativity is analogous to the old women of Africa who get a piece of root, chew it well, inundate it with spittle, then regurgitate it into a bowl and call the result food.

They are foremost among those who have never been able to see anything unusual in Kafka's "Metamorphosis", and why should they? —having been insects all their miserable lives. They will not thank you for confusing them with facts and for torturing them with truths; they have given up trying to convert you, so now they will crucify you. Those who know which side butters their bread realise that aesthetes must be anaesthetized not electrified in these enlightened days, and that on no account must they be urged to be functional, otherwise of course, the computer will blow a couple of gaskets.

My friend Gareth, who managed to get down to your place finally, apparently enjoyed your company immensely, and was very impressed with your work and of course with your motivation. As you probably gathered, he is deep in the language issue, but not to the degree where he allows emotion to cloud his political expertise, which is very acute. The Welsh Language has become the language of the Revolution due to the judicious direction of those like him, and to the horror of the dinosaurs who are cultural nationalists. Luckily matters have (thanks to the usual over-reaction of the establishment) gone beyond the stage where the dinosaurs could stop the bandwagon; anyone now who is able to synthesize both cultural and political aspirations into a coherent and literate policy, will be able to set the stage for the final act. The only factor required, apart from the catalyst who will weld emotion to intellect, is an economic recession of a degree which will also affect England equally (thus removing the ancient escape valve). This will get the man in the street, on the streets, because even those who do not love, or exercise logic must eat and provide. The lever of economic survival will then be exercised against the forces of re-action on behalf of the forces of innovation, and may that day come soon, because when it does, the true friends of Cymru will be recognised (as indeed they are now −to their detriment).

The struggle is naturally a political one, concerning, as it does, power and priorities, but things are not that simple and there are a whole series of concepts and principles involved, applicable to decency, civilization, culture, artistic matters, values and a way of life. The choice is between a field of corn and a factory producing "Country Maid" bread; it is between a man, sweaty feet and armpits, and a pre-packed, pre-digested, pre-conditioned consumer unit who confuses creation with pro-creation and who believes that choice means 'Coronation St.' or 'This is your Life'. British Democracy means freedom to rattle one's chains, and Law and Order guarantee that freedom. Socialisation has come to mean the opposite of its original meaning; it once meant the process by which one lost a little personal freedom and gained public toleration. Now it means wearing blinkers like medals and shining up one's leg irons proudly.

There must be a return to other, simpler, more true values, applicable to balanced happy mankind rather than to the Ford Assembly line. I expect you will have heard that there is an exhibition of my work in the Tregaron Arts and Crafts Centre. I only heard recently and I am amazed by the whole thing, because as an artist I am less than pedestrian, but I think the attraction is that instead of being fashionable, I have delved into Celtic Art which is a very esoteric subject not conducive to chocolate boxes or postage stamps, and one which goes right back into the racial subconscious. It appears that the "experts"

94

are hailing them as "Superb examples of Celtic Art" and yet I did half of them before I knew anything at all about the subject. It surprises me that of all Welsh artists, not one of them produces anything (to the best of my knowledge) recognisably Welsh —but there, perhaps they know which side of of their toast carries the caviar. In my ignorance however, I recognise one fact and that is that Celtic Art represents a glorious fusion of your particular gods, Pythagoras and Taliesin. I suspect that this form of art remains unrecognised for the same reason as Twm or indeed Taliesin, namely that their recognition would remove the basic prop for the justification of the 'civilising' influences of our imperialist masters.

Thank you for your kind and encouraging words; your psychology is good and very effective. Remember me to *my* masters. Hwyl.

Er mwyn Cymru,
John

To Sara Erskine

Annwyl Sara,

I hope that you, Ned and the children are in health and are happy.

Thank you for the Planets 22 & 23 and for the letter which accompanied No. 22.

I was most gratified at reading the comments by Ned in 23; you are all most kind and understanding at a time when such qualities are a crucial need.

Your remarks about my doing well in the exams as I had caught the right tone turned out to be prophetic; for that particular essay on Emily Dickenson I used the formula and received top marks. What we on the Humanities course find as we go along, is that we tend to fall into the jargon even in ordinary conversation, to such a degree that the discussion of a film becomes an academic thesis; for a little while I was worried about it, then enlightenment dawned as I realised that this was the intention (or at least part of it) of those who had formulated the system. The whole socialisation process of higher education revolves around the creation of an elite with a different life style, privileges, work-load, speech manner and vocabulary —all this to help disguise the very pedestrian criteria adopted under a sanctified veneer. I'm afraid they will have to pull a few subtler strokes than these to catch me; I am very well aware that a BA in this capitalist society is a piece of paper enabling me to start off half way up a selected ladder, and with better material expectations which do not depend on my pectorals. It may well give me a broader insight but it also teaches me where not to look, that is if I accept their assessment of the qualities of a balanced personality —which of course I don't.

I must also express my gratification at the amazingly efficient press coverage of the panel Exhibition; I would never have believed that Llais y Sais would see fit to mention me in a nonvindictive manner. (Cynically, I suppose that the Editor feels that as long as I am holding a pen in one hand and a palette in the other, that I am thus prevented from holding other, perhaps less innocuous, objects.) Obviously he prefers to be the recipient of a menacing cartoon rather than a sinister cartoon. I was rather surprised that the 'Nation' did not follow suit, but on reflection, as there *is* to be an election before long . . . etc. etc.

There is one great service you could do for me, if you would be so kind Sara, and that is to finally lay the ghost of that hoary old chestnut which has been following me around for years. I refer to the myth that maintains my inability to spell Mudiad Amddiffyn Cymru at the conference of Journalists in Chester. The facts are these:- Harold Pendlebury and Ian Skidmore[1] asked me the name and spelling of the movement. I told them the name, and Emyr Jones, a journalist from the Wrexham Leader, undertook (due to his proximity to Pendelbury) to spell it. He did so and got it wrong by leaving out an 'F' in the middle, upon which *I* corrected *him* and gave the right spelling, which considering that *he* is a Cymro Gymraeg, puts an entirely different complexion on the matter. I would be pleased (and amazed) if those persons who deliberately continue putting out this old myth, would instead turn their attentions to something far more deserving of public attention, namely, why at a time of such intense public curiosity (equalled only by the lack of any accurate information), the full explanation contained in the interview *was totally suppressed*, and indeed, apart from the trial, has never been mentioned. It could have been because at time when the Blaid was being blamed for many happenings, this statement would, by completely exonerating the Blaid, have effectively removed a very useful stick. Or it could have been that the information therein, during the impending jollifications for the '69 Circus, would have been putting the piranha among the goldfish. It certainly was not because it was not good copy, and it will take a damn sight more than a BA to make me forget that evidence of decadence and corruption in very high places. Of course it couldn't happen here, and even if

---

[1] Harold Pendlebury, Ian Skidmore, Emyr Jones: Three journalists who interviewed John Jenkins in May 1968. See *To Dream of Freedom*, Chapter 21.

it did, it didn't —and they say that the Irish don't make sense!

But enough —this is supposed to be a Thank You letter and indeed that is what it really is. I am sincerely grateful for both your strenuous efforts on my behalf; it is good to know that there are those Socialist Patriots whose courage complements others' convictions. The one without the other is life without hope and death without dignity. With you there is yet hope for Freedom, Justice, and Truth. Hwyl a Hedd.

Er mwyn Cymru,

John

H.M.Prison
Albany
26 August 1974

To Robat Gruffudd

Annwyl Robat,

I hope that you, Elwyn and your families are well and happy.

Many thanks for the posters, which now adorn my wall; I hope that they will adorn the walls of many more cells in the future.

I have sent on by separate cover, an attempt at a "Saint's Page". As you know there are three main types of Celtic decorated pages – the illuminated Capital letter, the Carpet Page (all decoration, nothing else) and the Saint's Page. I do not suppose that you will be able to do much with it because it is coloured and also because I used gold and silver on it, but possibly you might be able to utilize it in some way. Anyway, feel free. When you have finished with it (or if you cannot use it) perhaps you would be kind enough to give it to Sara Erskine at "Planet" –she will know what to do with it.

I have been surprised lately to read the reports in Llais y Sais regarding my being 'selected' as the candidate for Brecon & Radnor by the W.R.P. particularly as I knew absolutely nothing about it beforehand, never having been approached previously. As a Republican I cannot possibly countenance the idea of swearing loyalty to the bitch and her minions, and as a person of integrity I could never lower myself to serve in the establishments which contain such degenerates as George Thomas and his rabble of traitors and quislings. It is bad enough having to mix with criminals although it is modified by the fact that I have no choice in the matter, but to hobnob voluntarily with the decadent dinosaurs who flaunt their power and their hatred in the same way that a baboon displays his red & blue backside, would be anathema to me. To be a Pilate is one thing; to be a Judas is another.

As for the latest speech by Emyr Llew,[1] I believe his logic to

---

[1] **Emyr Llew:** Emyr Llewelyn, President of Adfer, a cultural/political organisation devoted to the defence of "Y Fro Gymraeg" (the Welsh Heartland).

be as impeccable as his timing is execrable. I feel that *at this stage*, anything which militates against the unity of our nation is not merely negative but counter-productive. Cymraeg must be seen to be the language of the social revolution, not the discourse of a folk museum. The workers of the conurbations *must* be educated to equate nationalism with Socialism, and the Welsh language with the avant garde of that movement. Any implication to the contrary, however sincerely made and felt is playing right into the hands of the traitors and quislings. I share the same feelings regarding culture and the future of Cymraeg as Emyr Llew, and possibly I would be prepared to go to the limits to see to it that the future is safeguarded beyond anything the opposition could attempt to sabotage the project. But this action can only be undertaken by a Welsh State by virtue of the fact that culture is a factor bound up with the economy and therefore political in the true sense of the word. Of course there *must* be a heartland, a power base for the culture, but until our State *is* established —and it can only be established with the consent of the majority of our people —the basic moves to establish such a power base must be made in such a way as to produce the maximum benefit with the minimum of friction. It is not so much a matter of priorities —I am not suggesting that the language question should be shelved in the interests of unity, because it is too important for that type of strategy; but it *is* a matter of discretion and timing and very much tied up with the adage about the wise old bull who decided to *walk* into the field and woo *all* the cows. Some of the ideas I have, and have held for some time, would make Emyr Llew's suggestions as socially disruptive as the Bishop's comments at his proverbial garden party; the name of the game is success for the cause and the strategy to be adopted is the one which will ensure this. If one wants a man dead, one does not perform a war dance and snarl at him; one smiles at him, gets behind him and slips a knife into him, as a result of which the man is dead and one is alive. Emyr Llew does not have to compromise his principles, but simply change his strategy. He need not say things he does not mean, but it is a simple matter of *not* saying what he *does* mean. There is no earthly reason why he, and others, cannot work to lay the foundations of the cultural power base in the same way as Cynog and Adfer. He does not have to do any huffing and puffing; just let him get on with building the new house —*I* will blow the old one down in due course if necessary, and if the people wish it. The language question is not a cultural one, but a political one, and it must therefore be approached in a political manner which means that every move envisaged must first be assessed on the important criterion of the political repercussions. A Pyrrhic victory for us in our state must be a loss; an established State without a soul is as sterile as a heartland with no political power. We must harness our love and our energy into a motivating force rather than a polarising factor; this should not inhibit our freedom of action but it *should* remind us that we walk a tightrope to reach our objective —and there is no safety net. From me this is good —but the approach must be catalytic, not cataclysmic.

Er mwyn Cymru,
John

To Sara Erskine & Ned Thomas

Annwyl Sara a Ned,

I hope that you and yours are well and happy.

Many thanks for your kind letter which I fully appreciated; I was pleased that you received the final manuscript. In fact I have sent one more drawing on, addressed to Y Lolfa in case they wish to utilize it but with instructions to Robat that it is be forwarded to you eventually. It is my first attempt at the classic "Saint's Page" and if you like it, please accept it with my thanks for all your much appreciated efforts on my behalf. The central figure is not terribly original, that being quite impossible due to the strictly formalised style of the period (as with Egyptian figures) but all the rest of it, is. Anyway I hope you like it, and that you will bear with my fumbling attempts, which I believe are generally acceptable only because the general public are not aware of the rules.

My mother was greatly impressed by the hospitality she received from Dafydd —she spent two pages lauding it, (and two lines on the exhibition, which is a tribute to her sense of priorities).

And now to the meat of this letter. I have been asked by an organisation called Mudiad Gwerin Cymru to allow them to nominate me as a candidate for Caerffili at the coming election. There are many factors involved and I am only aware of some of them because by being here I am clearly out of touch. I never make decisions on matters which do not lend themselves to value judgements, and so I am asking for your guidance, in all humility. My points are these:-

a) I do not know much about the Mudiad Gwerin Cymru. By accepting the nomination, I shall be giving them carte blanche to use my name —Do they have sufficient political acumen to run a constructive political exercise? Or will they attempt to tear down the Blaid for the sake of trendy dogma?

b) Will this business split the Nationalist vote? Does the long term interest of Cymru require that the vote *should* be split?

c) I am given to believe that the Blaid has lost its way and is not a politically Socialist-motivated movement, as much as a capitalist-undertoned cultural "Back to the Land" attempt by "local" Tories to exploit the natural desires of the people. I can hardly believe this, but I would like your opinion.

d) I, perhaps selfishly, certainly cautiously, do not wish to devalue the currency of martyrdom by placing it in the hands of money changers of whom I know next to nothing.

e) The M.G.C. have fairly stated that the seat will be fought on "Classic Republican abstentionist lines" of which I approve, because even if the miracle happened I would never consent to mix voluntarily with scum like Geo Thomas and his rabble of traitors and quislings. They also state that the object is "To give Plaid Cymru a kick in the right direction". Is this constructive in the circumstances? They seem, not to be anti-Blaid, but anti-Blaid's present policies.

There are many other factors involved and you will be as familiar with them as am I. I have great respect for your political acumen, but before giving me the decision I wish you to note one fact above all else:- The primary consideration is *not* to be based on *my* welfare, on *Plaid* policy or on *M.G.C.* requirements, but on the long term interests of Cymru a Chymry. If these interests coincide with Plaid policy, please tell me. I must admit that my instinct tells me to refuse outright, but I will not commit myself to a course of action on instinct alone. I have received a kind letter from a good friend who wants me to repudiate the M.G.C. "Because of the members' life styles" (presumably they drink and whore —openly!) and who hints that the "enormous prestige and support" I enjoy would cease, were I to condone such unseemly behaviour. Do I, in fact enjoy this support? And is it based on moral considerations?

Anyway, their letter requests an early answer, so I urge you in your capacities as friends and observers of the political scene, to give me your guidance soonest. I have tried to complete a fairly scientific analysis based on the newspapers and periodicals I have here, but I find it difficult to compute a line of action for someone who appears to be a synthesis of Frankenstein, Father Christmas, Genghis Khan, Dewi Sant, the Thing from the Swamps, and the keeper of the Holy Grail. You have both consistently helped and supported me in the past, and this gives you the right to guide me at this crossroads. My wish is to be analytic and catalytic rather than catalysmic and catastrophic; I feel that unity is preferable at this stage, to polarisation, and I would not wish to be part of the power base of a possible bunch of cowboys* (if indeed they are that). Please advise me Ned and Sara, I would be most grateful. Hwyl a Hedd.

Er mwyn Cymru,
John

* Some of whom seem to be nice chaps. One or two are friends.
J.   J.

To Raymond & Kitty Edwards

Annwyl Raymond a Kitty,

I hope that you and the boys are well and happy.

I am sending this brief note in answer to your latest letters (for which many thanks) so that you may know the position regarding the nomination for candidature. The fact is that I wrote to Gareth ap Siôn on 6th Sept to decline the nomination for the Caerffili seat; I am afraid that the piece you read in the Mule was evidence, not of my attitude to the nomination but of my diplomacy in approach. Perhaps I rather overdid it, but my personal philosophy dictates that I act only as ruthlessly as the occasion demands, and in this case, to be hurtful would have been to be arrogant. In point of fact, the day before anything at all appeared in either the "Guardian" or the Mule, I wrote to Eileen Beasley making my position quite clear. I said then, that if I were unable to *help* the Blaid, that I would certainly not *hurt* it. I was never approached regarding Brecon & Radnor at all, and only heard from the Mudiad Gwerin Cymru about two weeks ago; in the meantime yourself and a friend called to say exactly the same thing, and there were followed by another letter from Ned Thomas repeating the warning. Between us, there was never really a possiblity that I would consider their nomination —I am no politician but I am well aware of the lack of strategy involved in sacrificing a long-term objective to a short-term interest, particularly when the short-term interest has long-term effects and is not interesting anyway. In any case, in any matter like this, I never take action without carefully considering the ultimate effect on the Cymry and in particular, those who have done so much to help and support me and the Cause, over the years. If my destiny involves being a wedge then I must accept it; but I will not be a party to the ancient and fatal Cymric weakness of nit-picking, hair-splitting and faction-farming, in the face of a situation that demands unity above all else. The time to discuss the number of angels capable of accommodation on a pin-head, will no doubt come;

but we must not cease fighting the fire which is consuming our very foundations, to discuss it.

On the other hand, in the interests of *ultimate unity*, there must always be a bridge, a means of rapprochement available and acceptable to all sides. Which is why I chose to be diplomatic and not to alienate —need I say more! The fact that Cartimandua felt she had more in common with Rome than with Caradoc, illustrated a trait which we must eliminate if we are to survive this century intact. The best of Rome lives on, although under siege, but the worst of Cartimandua thrives and is encouraged and indeed is put forward as an example to the rest of us. There is no doubt an area of common ground suitable to both Cartimandua and Buddug; but getting them to that area could not be accomplished by addressing the one as a traitorous whore, and the other as a bloodthirsty bitch. *Sometimes it is better to mince words, particularly when the alternative is to mince men.*

As for Emyr Llew, I feel that the time to tell us about the necessity of building and maintaining the Heartland, is *after* he has built and maintained it. A few more speeches like that and we will not require religious differences to bring us into line with Ulster. The result will be a victory for Cymraeg, that is if you consider the large proportion of gravestones reading "Er Cof Am", over those that read "In Memory Of" to be a victory. He speaks from his heart, but he should filter the message through his brain, because in his position he must be a Statesman rather than a man.

Many thanks for your efforts on behalf of the exhibition at Tregaron; I did see it in the Mule (and was amazed). In the meantime, along with many others here I entered the "Koestler Award" scheme by submitting a few cards, including a print of the last Christmas one. I was surprised to find that they were considered good enough to exhibit and indeed I won a small cash award as well as the prestige involved in having a work accepted (there were 2 of us here accepted)..

Thanks also for arranging the "Mule" and the "Leader" which the newsagent according to regulations sends me every week, 'wara teg.

106

I was delighted to hear that you attended the Abergele ceremony this year and that you met Vida. There is no doubt about it, she is a very live wire and a very good friend to Cymru and myself. As for your query, regarding the action you should take to counteract all those statement issued by the M.G.C. I should be inclined to leave it. If they do not issue my statement in which I "regretfully" decline the nomination, then the lists will demonstrate the fact when they are published. If, in the meantime you wish to let the "Pobl Iach" know what is happening, quietly and privately, then please feel free; I have always felt that a pint tasted rather better on a Sunday morning around the back, alongside the local "Heddlu".

Many thanks again for your help; I very much appreciate your sincere motivation in helping me. Please give my love to the lovely children of your house and you know you have my best regards. Hwyl a Hedd.

Er mwyn Cymru,
John

To Sara Erskine

Annwyl Sara,

I hope that you, Ned and the children are well and happy.

Many thanks for your last three letters, & the Planet 24/25 which gets better and better (except that the factual articles tend to freeze my blood. The one about Regional Planning by Michael Geddes was Kafkaesque in its bland reiteration and normalcy in its deliverance, of the terrible and damning facts. Waking up to find one is a monster is one thing, but waking up to find that one is being eaten by one is something else). You will, of course, have guessed that along with that isotenic recluse Emily Dickinson, I found myself looking through the bars at Kafka; I am now wondering whether there are *any* "normal" authors. (With respect to you and Ned.)

I was very pleased when Ned so promptly squashed that strange chap James who wrote to the "Nation"; it seems a pity that people like him feel that clearing the deck for action includes shooting one's own side.

I join with you in a growing disquiet about the increasing dilution of the SNP by those who scent power and profit. When it becomes clear to the Scottish people that their new leaders are preparing to man the bunkers on the grouse moors rather than the barricades, then the bubble will burst, (and those too close will feel the splash I'm afraid). Glencoe, like Aberfan, is not so much the name of a place, but the description of an attitude and a life-style, because they represent collectively, not the results of the actions and inactions of bumbling or mistaken individuals, but the inevitable result of a system as ruthless as it is sophisticated.

•As for this business of having candidates everywhere, or concentrating resources on likely spots, I have always believed in the latter. The Blaid insists that their researches prove that their image improves with time, but I would like to see some concrete evidence of this: I cannot see what a constant loss of deposit proves, except an inclination to ignore reality. If indeed, the strategy involves getting MPs elected, then the success of half-a-dozen vulnerable seats, as the result of a concentrated campaign would do far more for the overall image of a thrusting successful party than what is presently happening. In their worrying over a possible loss of face, they are taking action which ensures just that eventuality. Not only is the Emperor wearing no clothes —that is fairly acceptable: but he is not yet the Emperor, and only a millionaire can afford to dress like a tramp, (if you will forgive the mixed metaphors).

Thank you for your very kind comments on the picture: I am very gratified that you accepted it and I hope you enjoy looking at it as much as I enjoyed drawing it for you. I must admit that I toyed with the idea of asking Robat to use it as the original for my Christmas cards this year, but that would have been a cheek, so I have produced another (different) one and sent that to him. I can only apologise for the quality of the paper, but I am a novice on all this sort of thing and am finding out the hard way about surfaces and hardness etc. I have been inspired by the rather unexpected reaction of people to what is after all, although traditional, a highly stylised form of art; it seems to touch a chord and to provoke a sympathetic appreciation of our heritage. At least I hope that is what is happening! There is nothing terribly original about an 18th Century Coach or indeed a Robin on a snowy branch; neither, of course is there anything original about the Dirk-Handle twist, Key Patterns, spirals and trishels —but they are *ours* and are peculiar to *us*, unlike the Coach & Robin, which would be as typical of Harrogate as of Hanover and Hamtramck USA.

You ask about the money from kind friends who wish to encourage me[1]. I hope you won't think me oafish if I ask you to send it to me here. I greatly appreciate the immense trouble to which you have subjected yourself, and I know you will understand when I tell you that my needs are many and my resources few. My children are young and my parents are old, and I have a good idea of the cost of living even though I am cut off from life.

---

[1]**kind friends who wish to encourage me:** These words were written above the words 'the sale of the pictures' which were deleted in order to comply with prison regulations.

I really should apologise for allowing the picture to be used in the new book about the Welsh Republic, without consulting you about it. I didn't think you would mind, but on reflection, I went about is the wrong way, and I am sorry.

I am presently shattered having on 5th & 6th sat the O.U. Exams on Humanities and on Personality Growth and Learning. Next year two full credit courses on the Renaissance & Reformation and The Age of Revolutions, so God help me. Anyway Calvin, Luther, Layola, the de Medicis and Borjias will come as a nice change to dear Emily, Kafka and Lawrence et al. My sincere regards to you all. Hwyl.

Er mwyn Cymru,
John

1975

H.M.Prison
Albany
31 March 1975

To Raymond & Kitty Edwards

Annwyl Raymond a Kitt,

I hope that you and the boys are well and happy.

Please forgive the undue delay in answering so for this year, I have several reasons for the inexcusable behaviour but they all boil down to the fact that I am behaving monstrously to my friends, and assuming that they have inexhaustible patience. Thank you very much for the very well chosen books which I am still devouring, and for the equally well chosen calendar (which, thank Heaven was relevant to the time of year and is the cause of envious remarks by several of my Irish friends. They get things with hands clutching rifles and walls covered with barbed wire —hardly inspiring!)

Incidentally (or perhaps not) I found the Christmas fare on T.V. and radio most disappointing. I was hungering for the Sacred music which I seem to remember used to be played almost all day not so long ago, but the media tended to regard the festival as secular rather than sacred. Things were a little better over Easter which I always anticipate, I think, with rather more fervour than the other, perhaps because it is rather less amenable to the profit-making which attends Christmas, and certainly because it is more central to my belief and indeed to Christendom. Every year I find myself becoming less tolerant of the money changers, and more conscious of a sense of awe and reverence when faced with the facts of a Calvary as stark and terrible as it is magnificent in its concept.

I find that there are several factors which contribute to my attitude in this place, and they are a) Celtic Art which by its very nature is devoted to Christian expression. The more deeply

I delve into its roots, the more I want to delve. b) The Church itself which gives me a companionship. c) The Open University which has taught me a great deal about the nature of religion. The Tutor is a lady who is not only very gracious but a dedicated and practising Christian. d) The nature of prison itself, which allows not only philosophic contemplation, but the facility to observe at first hand the natures and life-style of the inadequates of all levels. One is able to see quite clearly what is missing in their lives, and to wonder at the unusual displacement activities which can be utilized by humankind because of this failure to relate and interact with society as sick and misguided as are they.

About the O.U. To date I have achieved a full credit in "The Humanities", and one in "Making sense of Society" at foundation level. I also achieved a half-credit at 2nd level in "Personality Growth & Learning" (which is an Education course supposedly for teachers as I discovered after I had started it). This year I am doing two 2nd level full courses "Renaissance & Reformation" and "The Age of Revolutions". Next year, which is my final one, I propose to do "War & Society" (a full course) and "School & Society" (a ½ credit Education course). I really wanted to do "The Early Roman Empire & the Rise of Christianity" as a ½ credit course next year, but I am advised that Socio-linguistics is the coming thing in education, so I will concentrate on that. I seem to get on quite well with purely education courses, and anyway, I am personally very interested in Socio-linguistics for reasons which will be obvious to you.

I find that this year, doing two 2nd Level courses requires a rather different technique to the foundation level approach. Last year we were given a certain amount of source material, invited to assume that the reader of the essays was totally ignorant, (and thus had to have explanations of everything) and allowed to write a long essay. This year, we are given a vast amount of source-material, (there are 40 set books alone), enormously complex essays but with a limit of 1,500 to 2,000 words. The emphasis now is on vast research, ability to select the relevant material, to summarise this in a reasonable mixture of style & content, and to carry out interpretative analyses. So really it is a comprehension test on a very high level with the

112

ability to apply deductive logic —this is where the parrot brains
drop out because the facts are, very cleverly, never enough,
although there are too many from which to select.

But I am sure you are bored by all that, so to answer your
letter. Yes, Thank you I am regularly receiving the Leader. No,
Rhodri is not yet at Rhydfelen; he will be starting there this
Sept. I believe. I had a struggle with his mother who wanted
him to go to Pengam Grammar. Yes, I agree with you that
the strangely similar all-Wales attitude of the L.E.A.s is very
disturbing and should be the object of the C y I G's attentions,
because it represents a far more sinister long term threat than
the inertia of a public corporation. Some things cannot be
bought and after a certain age cannot really be eradicated either.
My love & respect to Kitt and the children. Hwyl a Hedd.

Er mwyn Cymru,
John

To Robat Gruffudd

Annwyl Robat,

I hope that you, Elwyn and friends are well and happy.

I write to thank you for your letter dated 10th March, which I almost received yesterday. I apologise for not being in a position to answer it, but when it arrived, I was informed that it was going to head office for translation (which I found rather strange, because there are people here on the staff well able to cope). Anyway it came back finally, and I was informed yesterday that I could now have it; I refused to accept it on principle, because after 6 weeks wait there is not much point any longer. I have of course placed the matter in the hands of Dafydd El[1], and await the result. I could not inform you earlier because I was not told until yesterday who the letter came from. I hope there was nothing in it which required an answer, urgent or otherwise, but I know you will understand that I must confront an attack on my basic rights, as a matter of principle.

I was appalled to read of the attacks on the "Welsh Republic" (even though the spin-off may have done Y Lolfa some good — or at least I hope so). While agreeing that the author was somewhat impolitic in his clarity, nevertheless one must grant that his logic is faultless. When one constructs a model, one utilizes a knowledge of behaviour patterns; whether this close observation and keen analysis happens to conflict with what the Vicar said on Sunday is neither here nor there. The author's mind is like a computer and his results are obtained from the many facts available; to satisfy his many critics, he should have thought like a computer and written like a politician, in which case there would have been a bowl of pap suitable for the toothless wonders grazing round our half-built cenotaph. But everything is relative, and a good friend of the author should swiftly produce a book based on that shadowy period between the time the people indicate their support for Socialist Nationalism

---

[1] **Dafydd El:** Dafydd Elis Thomas Plaid Cymru M.P. for Meirionydd (1974-).

and the time it is achieved. That will make his book on the first 10 Years look like a weather forecast, and draw the yelping flocks of leather-lunged, rubber-toothed castrati, off on a new chase.

I was not impressed by Saunders' latest epistle on behalf of the language; I feel that he is saying the wrong things for the right reasons. The answer to the survival and revival of the language lies in the careful nurturing by a Welsh State, but in the transitional period between now and then, the objective is to win the hearts and minds of our Werin, most of whom are socialised into the semi-derelict culture of industrial Wales. I would suggest that one will not win their minds by telling them that Cymraeg is a direct link with Rome; it would be more effective and relative to their social situation to show them that it is the direct route to a real revolution. Our new State will not be born naturally as the result of a church-blessed marriage between sweet reason and goodwill; it will be the bloody result of a caesarian section which itself was the result of a rape by imperialism of inertia —the knife will be the language. But the realisation of the language as the means of revolution will be the surgeon.

History may be bunk but cultural nationalism is cock, unless it is accompanied by political power. I see the Welsh language in the short term, not as an end but as a means, which having been finally realised would, in the long term ensure both the end and the means, of places supreme in importance and dependent on, and related to each other in the scheme of things. I am perhaps being simplistic when I see the Saunders system resulting in all the Cymry saying in Welsh "We are slaves of the capitalist system"; I see the over-cautious "constitutionalist" system, resulting in all the Cymry saying in English "We are members of a Socialist State". What *I* want is all the Cymry saying in Welsh "We are members of a Welsh Socialist Republic". The action and timing required to bring *that* about will make the Pope's Rhythm method look like the changing of the guard.

Two things —if you are in touch with Miles would you tell him that I couldn't comment on the books in the time given because I was (and am) up to my eyes in two 2nd level courses, and with no women or drink to distract am unable to do anything but work.

You asked if I needed anything —I would greatly appreciate a 45 rpm record of the Marseillaise if you could lay your hands on one, and/or an Ankh. Regards to all. Hwyl a Hedd.

Er mwyn Cymru,
John

To Sara Erskine

Annwyl Sara,

I hope that you, Ned, and the children are well and happy.

Many thanks for your last letter and the copy of 'Calgacus' (which I and my 'Q' Celtic friends enjoyed very much indeed). I proffer my ritual, but nevertheless sincere apologies for this tardy reply, in the hope that you will be tolerant of my short-comings.

Ned was too kind in his definition of a literary stylist; he was quite right in my case —I never write enough, but I will try to be a little more regular in the future. I was very pleased by his article in 'Calgacus', and indeed by the political approach of the whole magazine which I thought successfully linked National-ism with Socialism. It was very refreshing to read of pure and practical Socialism being practised North and West of Hampstead. I constantly get the impression that on "The Day", when one looks around at the Barricades, the English Left will have left because they're English. This observation is not based on ethnic considerations, but on ethical qualities..

I realise even while writing it, that one should not generalise, particularly about people, because to try to reduce human behaviour to a scientific equation is an effort which, thank God, consistently fails. Nevertheless I feel that the English Left is very insular and parochial and centred solely on London; perhaps I have been unlucky, but nearly every one I have met has turned out to be a trendy, hanging with the trappings of fashion and using a strange jargon to illustrate very peculiar criteria regarding the Cause.

I expect you read of the amazing adventure of Major Boothby whose name perhaps rings a bell? My 'Q' friends and I were intrigued to read of a new book called "The Angry Brigade" which purports to be all about "Britain's first Urban Guerilla Group"; it made us wonder whether perhaps we had made some mistake and had really been acting on behalf of the Girl Guides or the RSPCA. Certainly, if the blurb be true, we are being held under false pretences, and could not possibly have committed the political acts with which we were charged. Or perhaps because the acts did not happen in London, they didn't happen at all.

I expect that you will know of my recent removal from the 'A' Category. This came about as the result of a campaign in which I was greatly helped by Dafydd El and it has proved to me that if an MP is prepared to push and does not belong to the 'Club', even in these days it is still possible to get something done. Naturally, being a political decision, it had nothing to do with right or wrong; they would lose a certain amount of control by removing me from the 'A' list, but they stood to lose a lot more by leaving me on. So they took me off, although with just one year to go anyway, they have not amazed me with their generosity.

I have as usual been trying to assess the political situation in Wales and I am impressed by two factors which strike me as very significant. The first concerns the consistent success of Nationalist candidates in local elections in the anglicised areas, and the second in the change (or apparent change) in emphasis on the part of the Cymdeithas to their role. They seem to be quietly but inevitably moving into the socio-political area rather than the purely cultural one; this may well remove some of the old reactionaries who have long viewed the unemployment graphs and the Welsh speaking totals as in no wise connected, but it will certainly attract an appreciative and practical group of sympathisers, and extend the catchment area.

I hope you are not yet totally surrounded by those who are trying to get away from it all by bringing it all with them. I also hope that the unfortunate 1320 Club has not upset or set back the Cause in Alba. I have tried to find out here, how the political situation is looking in Scotland, but the Scots I speak to, all seem to be very familiar with Arsenal and Spurs, and they don't appear to know anything about the Gaelic Language Society or indeed about Scotland. Perhaps I have met the wrong people. My very best wishes to you all. Hwyl.

Er mwyn Cymru,
John

H.M.Prison
Albany
11 December 1975

To Vida Herbert

Annwyl Modryb Fida,

I hope that both yourself and Adela are well and happy.

Many thanks for your letters, which I always find most helpful and informative; thanks also for the cheque which was a
very kindly-meant gesture and which was received with gratitude
for your thoughtfulness.

I was pleased that you received the parcel of Celtic Art intact,
and I really should have sent a small note with it to explain the
contents. It contained, in fact, the two certificates and the
works which won them. The three cards mounted on the board
were responsible for the 1974 certificate, and the poster,
Christmas card and Dewi Sant illustration, for the 1975
certificate. The card I have designed for this Christmas has not
arrived yet from Y Lolfa but it should be on the way by now.
When it was time to submit work for this year's Koestler award,
I did not even have one single 1974 card left, so I appealed to
the Education people here to return the one I had given them,
for inclusion. They did not mind, and I was able to paint it,
(which, owing to the lateness of arrival last year, I was unable to
do with yours, I fear) and eventually forward it to you. This
perhaps will explain the rather formal message inside the card,
and the card I will send you this time will be less formal as be-
fits our relationship.

Thank you also for the beautiful cards, and Christmas card,
which you kindly sent; they are much appreciated, as much for
their beauty of content as the pureness of thought which motivated their sending. I am very touched also, by the folder which
I find extremely useful in my work —many thanks again.

I agree entirely with your very perceptive assessment of the
"Socialist Worker". I have noticed in the past that like certain
so-called Welsh MP, the articles support every minority except
their own. They simply will not admit to the existence of a
Welsh Identity with aspirations outside the terms of their
personal experience, and as our whole raison d'être as national-

119

ists, is based on this identity, we cannot ever even begin our dialogue on a rational basis. If they would ever admit that I were right in my assessment, it would mean to them only the loss of an "academic" argument and a gain in practical experience; but if I should ever admit that they were right, to me it would mean the total collapse of my whole life force, and complete moral and spiritual suicide. But of course they can never realise this simple fact, and therefore we can never argue and discuss in a mature and rational manner.

I feel that basically the Welsh concept of life in its broader aspects, differs considerably from the urbane and cosmopolitan version postulated by our masters as being the peak of perfection. That terrible experiment by Professor Limbardo which proved conclusively that man can be successfully moulded by his environment into practically anything desired by the manipulators, although dreadful, proves what we in Cymru have known for a long time. Are we then to be blamed for trying to create an environment which will bring out and encourage the *better* aspects of humanity, commensurate with our aspirations?

Why indeed should we be forced to assess people as consumer units, production units, and to look at homes as domestic units? There is more to life than statistics, and there is more to the soul than is possible to descirbe in a production graph. And how can the wonderful term "Pietas" ever be reduced to an equation? They want us to struggle in the mud when we should be in flight to the stars of our aspirations; their inspiration is the clinking of gold and ours is the ringing of nails. They are in thrall to beer and skittles; we are enthralled by milk and honey.

We must return to a new Celtic Church which is the Old Celtic Church, one in which simplicitas and pietas are given their rightful place. History tells us that the Welsh Early Christian Church was the last in these islands to submit to the domination of the Reformed Roman Church; let it be also the first to return to a condition of grace under the language of old Rome and the new "Pax Celtica". It is not simply a politico-economic struggle, but one of intense moral, ethical and spiritual motivation; but this is judged on *our* premises and 'they' will never understand that.

Perhaps this is just as well, because their ignorance is our greatest ally, and their intolerance our sharpest spur. My best wishes to all our friends and my sincere regards to you both. Hwyl a Hedd.

                    Er mwyn Cymru,
                    John

1975

H.M.Prison
Albany
4 January 1976

To Raymond Edwards

Annwyl Raymond,

Hawddamor! I hope that you, Kit and the boys are well and happy. I have just been reading the Mule of 17th Oct. and find its basic message the same ill-informed hotch-potch that one used to expect in the bad old days; it seems to be written not tongue-in-cheek but dummy-in-mouth, and one is inclined after careful analysis and systematic scrutiny, to murmur "Diddums then".

I find two words rather puzzling in their context; they are "Violence" and "Democratic Society". I recollect some time ago, in those letter columns, a letter from a bomber pilot, who during the war had inadvertently killed children; he now found his conscience bothering him and asked someone for justification of his actions. It soon came from some airforce person, who told him that he was only following orders and they absolved him from any personal responsibility. So apparently "they" give you a uniform, and you give them your conscience! And it follows that anything you do is *not* violence because the State allows it and indeed demands it. It therefore appears that violence is only violence when it is not condoned by the State, and that the action alone is morally neutral, until measured by motivation. So if, as a result of someone signing a piece of paper, I am sent to Cyprus and there kill some "political undesirables", I am a hero; but if on returning to Cymru I am motivated by my conscience, and attempt to assist the Cause in a dramatic manner, then I am an evil criminal. Is one then to

---

[1]Mule of the 17th Oct.: See *Western Mail* editorial 17.10.75 'Bombers in the halls of fame'.

accept that the State and not the Lord is the arbiter of morality? And is legality the only measure of morality and duty?

In Abergele there is a Chapel, the trustees of which have refused to allow a dignified and seemly annual service of commemoration in respect of two patriots. Their reason is apparently that these men were "Men of violence"; one wonders what their attitude would be if the son of a member were killed in Ulster whilst on active service. Would they refuse a commemoration service on the grounds that as a member of the armed forces, the person was a "Man of violence"? It seems that in this democratic land, those who own the mint have produced coins with Caesar's head on both sides and that those who should know better, abet them. I will say of that chapel only this —if in 100 years time the God worshipped there is venerated in the language used there today, it will not be due to the attitude and approach of those who presently inhabit it. Palm Sunday Christians make good mourners but poor martyrs; their God performs miracles which offend no one, he *never* breaks the rules by violently attacking those who have defiled the Temple. Luckily for our beloved land and the Cause, there are many other Chapels and many other ministers who are able to see the whole situation in its proper historical context, and who see Christianity in its proper social perspective. Religion, as practised by Palm Sunday Christians, is indeed the opium of the people, seeking as it does to disengage the moral regulator from the State-geared engine; true Chritianity applies the precepts of Him who saw two sides to a coin, to practical politics, thus acting as a spur to progress.

I am unable to comprehend the statement that "It is astonishing and saddening that pacifists have succeeded in performing the intellectual somersaults necessary to land them in Mr Jenkins's camp". The pacifists and myself have always agreed on the basic premises of the Welsh condition, the reasons for it, its fatal destination in the circumstances obtaining, and the crucial need for radical reform; we have always disagreed on the lengths to which one should go to achieve this radical reform. Inevitably and invariably, every letter I have ever received from these people, contains a statement to the effect that they entirely disagree with my methods as they understand them, and this is as it should be. They have not joined my camp and neither have I, because I do not have one. They respect me for my single-mindedness and my dedication to the Cause, and I respect them because they are equally inflexible and totally fair in the application of their principles —they would no more dream of becoming a Freedom fighter than they would of becoming a State-sponsored terrorist. They are inflexibly hard and this is acceptable because they are totally committed to an abstract ideal which recognises only morality and a very Christian morality at that. They recognise the morality of the Cause, and although they themselves could never condone the actions undertaken by activists, they realise that in non-pacifist eyes, those actions are the lesser of two evils. Paradoxically, their ideals are those for which we fought, but there is a place for both of our people; some are needed to worship at the shrine and others must guard the gates. Mea Shearim[2] would not appreciate the rumble of Israeli tanks on the Sabbath, but it is due to the concepts kept alive by Mea Shearim that the tanks are there to go out —and it is because of the tanks that Mea Shearim will survive to maintain those concepts.

It is possible that I took the wrong road; but it is difficult to see through eyes blinded by tears and the sublime radiance of the Holy Grail. It is also difficult to comprehend how this experience can be compared in any way with the exploits of the train robbers, who were simply materialist fleas on a materialist dog, but as the Mule insists on bringing the comparison up, perhaps it could be used to illustrate the difference between our motivations and subsequent actions and to define the difference between a politically motivated activist and a criminal. A criminal commits a crime to the detriment of society and for his self-interest; a political activist performs actions detrimental to his self-interest and for the benefit of society. If there are those establishment figures who still maintain that there is no difference between myself and a train robber, and that in any

---

[2]**Mea Shearim:** (Heb. Hundred Gates). The quarter of Jerusalem that is inhabited by Eastern European Jews who do not recognise the State but continue to expect the restoration of Israel with the advent of the Messiah.

case there are no political prisoners in this country, then let him consider this fact. Had I and the train robbers performed our respective functions in Northern Ireland (which is, of course an integral part of Britain), then I would be, after conviction, placed in a separate prison from those; I would be allowed to wear my own clothes, I would receive special visits and receive all the privileges of a prisoner with political status. Would they?

I must however, agree entirely with the Mule, "That the use of violence to achieve political objectives in a democratic society is an intolerable and inexcusable strategy." It therefore logically follows that the use of violence to achieve political objectives in a non-democratic society is a tolerable and excusable strategy. While admitting that this *is* a non-democratic society, I deny that I used political violence. The term "violence" when defined by the dictionary involved the "Quality of being violent" as the "Unlawful exercise of physical force". Certainly, as understood by the majority of people, the expression implies the "Deliberate application of physical force against people with intent to kill or maim", and this is something against which our collective faces were as inflexibly turned as my pacifist friends'. The police made a big production of the fact that it had cost £7 million to put me in the dock at Yr Wyddgrug; it is then credible that with a campaign that long and apparently successful, that the untoward incidents involving people were planned? Are people really expected to believe that the many instances which occurred of the symbolic destruction of, and damage to buildings and installations were successful, but that no-one was hurt in any way was a pure fluke?

One thing the Mule may care to mull over is the fact that the public has a right to know, which, in a democratic society, has priority over what certain cabals feel should be made public. In the '60's as I recall, the columns of certain newspapers almost totally ignored facts which were crucial to the Welsh Public's ability to assess the situation and reach a conclusion. A dramatic incident or two involving damage, may well be considered a rather extreme method of drawing attention to, for instance, the rapaciousness of large conurbations wanting water, and the impotence of, and indeed lack of, any machinery capable of demanding justice. But, due to the rather clever bias, half-truths, and total censorship being exercised, was there any other way? Certainly, by the late '60's, most Welsh people knew all about Tryweryn, Fyrnwy, and other anachronisms; they were also well aware that there was very considerable opposition to the Caernarfon circus. Naturally they would not know very much of the freedom-fighters involved in the direct action, because although a full statement had been made to eminent journalists, explaining the aims and motivation of the organisation, this was suppressed by a certain cabal, who although well aware of the lies involved, found it more expedient to continue to smear the official Nationalist Party (and indeed still do) with blame for the incidents.

As this letter shows signs of becoming an epic, I shall endeavour to get down to earth again. I would remark, however, that I do *not* require (as the Mule puts it) the compassion of people of my country. It is a sad commentary of the times when one who is totally committed to his country and who has geared his abstract concepts to concrete practicalities, is felt to be in need of this pity. I feel that our talents are God-given and that we were placed here to exercise them. Such as I had, I exercised. I paid my debt to the society in which I was born, during the years '66-'69; I am now paying my resulting debt to the English State, and I exult in having been given the wonderful opportunity to help my poor country. I have become used to being misunderstood and deliberately misrepresented, but I realise that my good and true friends are working hard to rectify this.

Many thanks indeed for your letters and the excellent books you were kind enough to send me at Christ Mass; also for the 'Leader' contribution which heartened me greatly.

As for my work on release, I have nothing concrete in mind. I may go in for a post-graduate course eventually at Cardiff involving the Journalism diploma they run down there because, quite frankly, there are no offers of employment; I will have to play it by ear on gaining freedom. (Perhaps we could discuss?)

Yes, there would now be no possible objection to your visiting (except that this is quite a dreadful place to get to and from, unless you could manage to stay for a day or two), now that I am on the 'B' list. Please let me know when you would like a Visiting Order and I will send one post haste.

Presently, I await the OU '74 results with some trepidation. Rhodri is established at Rhydfelen and is reportedly doing escellently. I receive the 'Leader' regularly but could not send a card to my benefactor —no address. I therefore take the liberty of enclosing one for you to hand him (and a couple more for any 'Fund' friends you feel should receive, —again, I have no adresses). There is one point, to do with my not mentioning the cottage to Audrey & Albert on their visit; it was because at the time I had heard nothing of it myself.

I really must close now, it is late on New Year's Eve, and in an hour or so I shall be able to tell myself that I shall be free this year. I am full of emotion because I have waited long for this day, and I am very mindful of the loyal and true friends who have helped to remove the bars from my window and the wire from the surrounding fence by keeping me in touch with *my* world.

I hope you like the card this year; I gather that some extreme protestant friends are not terribly keen, but Celtic Art *is* a spiritual and Catholic art, and I am not prepared to 'adjust' an old tradition in order to comply with comfortable expediency. Anyway, flexibility on basic issues was never one of my stronger points, thank God.

I look forward very much to seeing you all in the not too far distant future. In the meantime I wish you all the very best for the New Year and assure you of my most sincere regards and love.

Er mwyn Cymru,
John

To Fida Herbert

Annwyl Modryb Fida,

I hope that you and Adela are well and happy.

At last, free of the seasonal rush which occurs in even such places as this, I am in the right frame of mind to reply to your letters. Perhaps I should mention that the results of my last year's examinations came through yesterday and that I passed with good grades in both courses.

Many thanks for the two delightful books you sent; they will, apart from giving me great pleasure, also assist in the course of 3rd level study I am taking this year, "The 19th Century Novel".

I received many cards this year, one of the best ever, but more of that later in the letter.

You ask about the meaning of the card I created this year; the strange thing is that you are only the second person to realise that it is not just a pretty, coloured picture. You are quite right, there *is* a message, and more important —it is based on a letter I received from you earlier in the year in which you bemoaned the love of trappings rather than basic principles, and urged a return to the simple Celtic Church. I will begin with specific details: the gorgeously robed and decorated saintly priest on the left is shown in comparison with a simple lamb, and no matter how meek, mild or simple he can be, he will never be as meek and mild as the lamb. The soldier saint on the right is splendidly apparelled, but in comparison with the natural and gorgeous peacock (a product of nature) he can be seen as false and artificial. The peacock is perched on the holy "Tree of life", a product of pre-Roman, even pre-Egyptian Celtic heritage which goes back into the mists of our history. The plant is the mistletoe. The words 'Wele! Dyma'r Oen' could not be more simple, stark and submissive, yet they are totally submerged in a wealth of decoration so that the outlines can barely be seen. The great Wheel Cross, a symbol of brazen and barbaric torture and death, is likewise so involved in colour and decoration that, like a sword wreathed with May flowers, its basic function is barely evident. Mary the Mother is simple and unadorned; she stands in the international manner of submission, with Her hands open and extended to the world, as She offers us Her Son Of them all, the Christ Child is the simplest and starkest, uncoloured, undecorated with His hands in the gesture of a loving welcome to us. And more terrible, he occupies that very place on the Cross, where he will eventually receive our response to his welcome. The whole card as a concept pays generous lip service to beauty, but it screams aloud for a return to the basic principles and understanding buried beneath the adornments of centuries. We worship the Cross, but we have forgotten the Christ. Modern crosses have become decorative, dripping with diamonds and shining with silver; the original dripped with blood and tears and shone with sweat, and we must *never* forget this. The Archbishop of Wales has gone a long way since Dewi Sant pulled his plough without horses; perhaps it is time to retrace our steps to discover where we took the wrong direction. The Christ-Child, the Mother, the words, the lamb and the peacock are natural, simple and stark; their silent message is the antithesis to that purveyed by the wreathing and convoluted decorations and the glittering gilded cross with the splendidly adorned saints on either side. This is not to say that there should be *no* decoration of any sort, but it *is* to say that we sould carefully distinguish between the real and the artificial, between simple faith and love of ceremony. Love of beauty is an aid to devotion, not a replacement for it, and the truth in relation to the trappings should not be placed in the same position as the needle in the haystack. What I have tried to do with the card is to symbolize what 'they' have done with Christmas, except that I have made visual comparisons. Belief is beautiful, but beauty is not belief. Belief is not besmirched by beauty *but* it *is* based on blood, tears, sweat and a love as sweet as it was uncompromromising. We must return to our original priorities and not confuse the wrappings with the contents; both are necessary, but we must recognise the difference.

And that, Modryb Fida, is the card; thank you for the kind comments on it, and of course for the inspiration which created it.

Thank you also for "Y Drych" which I enjoyed. I thought your suggestion re the article on Celtic art particularly apt, but perhaps it would not be very seemly if I did it. As far as I know there are not many people who practise Celtic art and certainly not many who attempt to integrate it into modern life without losing sight of its basic rules. Therefore any such article would be virtually certain to contain some fleeting reference to myself, and I know you will understand that a critical assessment should, in order to be objective, be undertaken by another.

* * *

This Christmas, my seventh and last in prison, I received hundreds of cards to mark the occasion. I wish to offer my humble and grateful thanks to those many well-wishers and sympathisers who have supported me through nearly seven years; they will perhaps never realise how very much they have done for me and my beliefs. Those who visit me, inevitably remark that imprisonment seems to have left me untouched and unchanged, and while this effect is not uncommon on those motivated by political belief, it could only be achieved by the knowledge that one is supported by those who care. This knowledge is conveyed by gestures such as cards at Christmas, and while they cannot remove my bars and barbed wire, they make me immune to my surroundings. With friends such as these, my body may be imprisoned but my soul cannot be caged; my mental attitude in prison is dictated purely by the atmosphere projected by my friends. Thanks to my actions my feet are rooted firmly in the slime, but thanks to my friends, my eyes are fixed firmly on the stars. My sincere regards Modryb Fida (Many thanks for plans of garden lay-out) and Adela.

Er mwyn Cymru,
John

To Vida Herbert

Annwyl Modryb Fida,

I hope that you and Adela are well and happy.

Many thanks for your latest letters, which as is usual afforded me great interest and to which I always look forward with lively anticipation. I should perhaps mention here, that now our correspondence is officially sanctioned, the need to record their delivery is no longer as valid as it once was; I mention this only in order to save you undue bother and expense.

* * *

I expect you will have heard by now that R. came down to see me recently bringing with him another good friend L.H. I feel very angry when I think about poor D. (L's friend) because she teaches Cymraeg in a school staffed by indifferent and promotion-conscious teachers, and headed by a person who is savagely anti-Cymreig a Chymraeg. This Head is constantly denigrating D's department and always trying to sabotage its work both socially and politically, thus making her working life a misery and an uncertain one at that. Like some of these preachers you have mentioned, Philistines like this Head will doubtless meet their just deserts in due course, although when that time comes, no doubt like the types they are, they will have long gone to retire in a grateful England.

The English establishment owes these traitors and quislings a great deal, and demonstrates this fact when the honours and appointments are made. Be sure, Modryb Fida, that the reason why you will never be mentioned in the honours list for the work you have done for Wales, is that you have worked for Wales. I was naïve enough to be surprised in 1969 when a certain Lance/Corporal in the Royal Engineers received a minor honour for his work in aid of Welsh culture; in fact he had helped to design the layout of the Army Camp housing the bulk of the troops assisting in security for the investiture. Welsh culture! But again, if it can be said of George Thomas' elevation to the Speaker's Chair, that it was "A great day for

Wales", there is nothing that can surprise us, used as we are to the double-talk of those with double standards and devious strategy in the achievements of their fatal objectives. I do not object to their being traitors, quislings and careerists of the worst sort; what I detest thoroughly is the spurious morality they lay on as thickly as the make-up on a madam (and for the same reason). I cannot object to their existence and methods, for such creatures have always been with us; dogs have lice, flowers have fungus, and we are saddled with *"them"*. The hypocrisy is what sickens me, and in the final analysis, it is this aspect of their treachery which will overwhelm them.

* * *

Yes, I very much enjoyed meeting Nansi Richards and Elfed Lewis some years ago; she has a very restful and sympathetic personality, and I remember noting to myself at the time that she personified the very real aspects of Cymru a Chymreictod for which I was fighting, and which it was so necessary to protect and succour if life were to mean anything more than an undignified and grasping journey between womb and tomb. There was an impression of great simplicity and great ability, a good relationship between art and humanity, the memory of which has stood me in very good stead ever since. When I consider the ostensibly chance contacts and apparently random factors which have combined to make me what I am, then I must praise the God who has so carefully passed the ammunition. There is more to us than consumer and producer units travelling along on a mass-production line motivated by the fearsome engines of self-interest geared to a materialist generator. If that were so, then I would not be here and you would not be there and there would be no sympathy between us. I am sending you some more cards; do with them as you wish —keep them for next Christmas, enter them in the National —anything. My sincere regards to you both.

> Er mwyn Cymru,
> John

To Vida Herbert

Annwyl Modryb Fida,

I hope that you, Adela and all friends are well and happy.

Many thanks for all the letters, cuttings and indeed books with which I have been delightfully showered; what a difference the receiving of them makes to my usually tedious and mundane daily routine. And I always find the information so very relevant and useful for my studies which are proceeding apace.

But to answer your queries; yes I sent a card at Christmas to Professor J.Gwyn Griffiths at Abertawe. (Did you know that he is the father of Robat Gruffudd of Y Lolfa who printed the cards for me?) I must also mention that I sent no explanation to anyone in Cymru; there was only one person, apart from my University tutor, whose curiosity prompted her to ask, and that was an ex-Indian Missionary to whom I sent an an explanation. If you wish to send explanations to anyone, please feel free to do so; they will probably be glad to get them, but of course you will be far more able to judge that than anyone else.

I must admit to being a little surprised by the response to this last card; almost everyone expresses their liking for it and yet so very few question the symbolic figures. I am wondering whether this is the inevitable result of the present system whereby everything is mass-produced, designed to be neutral and bland, and the last quality expected is anything thought-provoking or even abrasive. The fact that something is produced for non-profit motives, and simply to mark a great Christian occasion, while making a personal statement, probably does not even register. So if you feel able to enlighten some our mutual friends, I will certainly be very pleased and so, no doubt, will they. The fact that people like the cards for their appearance alone, reassures me that I have gone some way towards bringing our ancient art-forms into a reasonable integration with contemporary expect-ations. The 'Wele' card is entirely due to your inspiration, be-cause you interested me in Celtic Art originally, and in the concept of simplicity and faith specifically relating to this card.

As to the technicalities and techniques involved in the transcribing of the concept to paper, I know it hardly seems reasonable but I must ask you to accept that my hands and senses seem to work on their own instinctively, as though I had extensive previous experience in these things.

* * *

My main problem at the moment is involved with obtaining employment in Cymru, and I am hoping that my situation will not parallel Saunders Lewis's, who, I gather, spent about fourteen years unemployed on his release from Wormwood scrubs. I know that times have changed, but the 'respectable' people are still with us and their bread is still buttered by the same people. It will be very ironic if I have to leave Cymru in order to work in England because 'our' people are afraid of me and what I represent, or perhaps because it pays them to be circumspect in these matters.

* * *

I agree with your critique of Daniel Jenkins' book entirely; he has been 'there' too long and his mind has a political rather than purely academic bias. This book, though good in parts, echoes too loudly the clink of his gold, so that one cannot hear the clank of our chains. My sincere regards to you both.

Er mwyn Cymru,
John

H.M.Prison
Albany
7 July 1976

To Vida Herbert

Annwyl Modryb Fida,

I have just received your letter No 5 and I am very worried because you do not seem to have heard that my release date has been put back one week to the 15th. I asked Watcyn to let you know, and I can only imagine that either his letter has gone astray or that it is taking along time to reach you. I am horrified at the thought of your expecting us ond the 8th and our not appearing; I hope the matter resolves itself.

* * *

Please forgive me for the brevity of this letter which I pen to try to catch the post in order to alleviate any worry on your part regarding my time and date of arrival. I will also have to crave your indulgence and understanding on my arrival, I fear, because I will be probably fatigued and harrowed. I know that you will understand and bear with me, and my knowlede of this will allow me to relax in a manner impossible while with others, who expect me to comport myself consonant with my reputation rather than my principles.

They should know by now that I am exactly the same as everyone else, except that, like you, my priorites are different.

I will write again to you, more fully next time. My sincere regards and respect to you both.

Er mwyn Cymru,
John

Finally, a book review of The Welsh Extremist *by Ned Thomas. This was published in the October 1-8, 1971 edition of* The Welsh Nation, *but was originally sent as part of a letter to Mr Gareth Miles.*

There have been more detailed books on the language and on politics, but Mr Thomas has avoided the cardinal error of viewing those subjects in isolation and has beautifully and naturally synthesized the two.

The one omission made by Mr Thomas is a detailed study of those like myself who are Welsh but not Welsh-speaking and English-speaking but not English.

This is a pity because these are the people who are going to determine the Welsh future because of their numerical preponderance.

Mr Thomas deals with the Cymro-Cymraeg and with the Cymro di-Gymraeg, but I believe he is not aware of the extra dimension of deprivation suffered by the latter (and there are many of them) which tend to drive them into an insane fury when the language is slighted in any way.

It is a highly significant fact that the two national Welsh Martyrs who died at Abergele were not Welsh-speaking, but I affirm that they truly loved the Welsh language. As a result of Mr Thomas's insight, we are now able to list the essential differences between the Welsh and the English. These are:

1. Culture, which in England is associated with income, class, type of education and accent. In Wales it is associated with the knowledge and love of the Welsh language, history and literature.

2. Class and tribalism. In England the only real and genuine contact between the classes takes place in the trenches and in bed, and these days it must be admitted that this contact between the classes no longer even seems to include the sexes.

In Wales the classes the criteria are significantly different and nationalism is highly developed.

In England, the people an area hold a big carnival to celebrate the fact that the new London airport will, instead of coming to their area, move away a few miles for its site.

How very parochial and tribal, and how impossible in Wales where all Welshmen would feel for the nation at a time like that.

3. Temperament. In England, the people are generally Conservative, noted for their intolerance to strangers and who are self-seeking.

In Wales, there is a willingness to die, a capacity for belief and a a potential for suffering and enduring, and a strong radical tradition socialism.

The military, political and economic ward have long been lost in Wales and the final cultural annihilation has been slowly, in-sidiously and fatally gathering momentum, whereas the violence that has resulted as the recognition of the danger to the life of the nation, has been instant and more easily visible in its effects. He agrees that the trouble with Wales today, in the face of the mindless and bureaucratic genocide practised by our masters, is caused by the activities of the extremists and nationalists; extreme Welsh Pacifism which seeks peace at any price and English Nationalist Welshmen. They will be the death of us if we we let them. There is an inescapable conclusion to the fact assembled with such feeling by Mr Thomas.

The anti-Welsh faction maintain that they will not cater for Welsh because it is not economically necessary due to bilingual-ism and they likewise make it clear that there will be no progress for our nation by normal means.

The answer is clearly to lie down and die or to get up off our knees and enforce monolingualism to make catering for Welsh an economic must, and if we are denied normal means to use any means compatible with the survival-as-Welshmen-at-all costs policy.

We do not make the rules but to survive we must find the answers, however nauseating to some, or we must accept our serfdom in perpetuity. They insist on regarding us as tribal, so they should remember that what they are taking from us is more than a member of the family.

They disparage our past, denigrate our present and deny us a national future by castrating our cultural vitality, excising our identity.

Er mwyn Cymru,
J.B.Jenkins (M.A.C.)

Also published by Y Lolfa

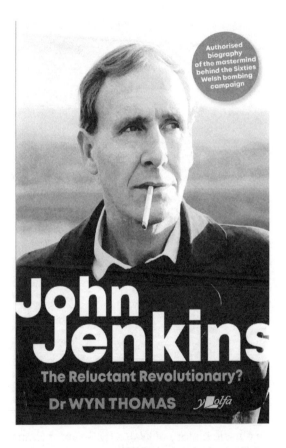

The full, authorised biography; 384 pages
in hardback.
£19.99

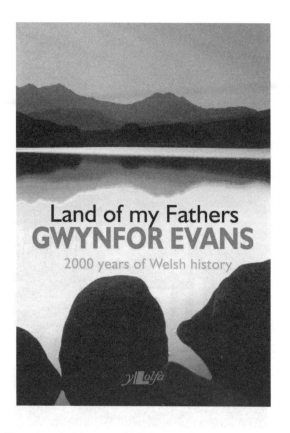

The classic history of Wales by Gwynfor Evans,
architect of the twentieth century Welsh
national revival.
£12.95

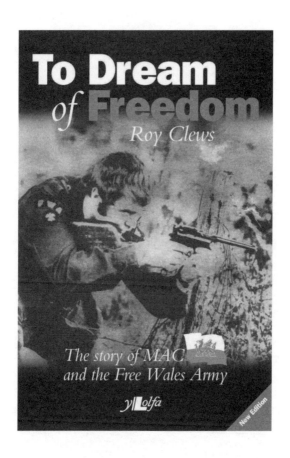

To Dream
of Freedom

Roy Clews

*The story of MAC
and the Free Wales Army*

y Lolfa

New Edition

The story of MAC and the Free Wales Army
grippingly told by Roy Clews.
£9.95

For a full list of our books of Welsh interest, go now to our website, **www.ylolfa.com,** where you may browse and order on-line – but support your local bookshop if you can.